T0325521

BASEBALL AMERICA PRESENTS

BEFORE THEY WERE STARS

SECOND EDITION

BASEBALL AMERICA INC. · DURHAM, N.C.

Baseball America

ESTABLISHED 1981

P.O. BOX 12877, DURHAM, NC 27709 • PHONE (919) 682-9635

EDITOR AND PUBLISHER B.J. Schecter *@bjschecter*
EXECUTIVE EDITORS J.J. Cooper *@jjcoop36*
Matt Eddy *@MattEddyBA*
CHIEF REVENUE OFFICER Don Hintze
DIRECTOR OF BUSINESS DEVELOPMENT Ben Leigh
DIRECTOR OF DIGITAL STRATEGY Mike Salerno

EDITORIAL
ASSOCIATE EDITORS Kegan Lowe *@KeganLowe*
Josh Norris *@jnorris427*
Justin Coleman *@ElJayColes*
SENIOR WRITER Ben Badler *@benbadler*
NATIONAL WRITERS Teddy Cahill *@tedcahill*
Carlos Collazo *@CarlosACollazo*
Kyle Glaser *@KyleAGlaser*
WEB EDITOR Mark Chiarelli *@Mark_Chiarelli*
SPECIAL CONTRIBUTOR Tim Newcomb *@tdnewcomb*

PRODUCTION
DIRECTOR OF PRODUCTION Linwood Webb
DIRECTOR OF DESIGN James Alworth

BUSINESS
TECHNOLOGY MANAGER Brent Lewis
ACCOUNT EXECUTIVE Kellen Coleman
OFFICE MANAGER & CUSTOMER SERVICE Angela Lewis
CUSTOMER SERVICE Melissa Sunderman

STATISTICAL SERVICE
MAJOR LEAGUE BASEBALL ADVANCED MEDIA

Alliance
>>>> BASEBALL <<<<

BASEBALL AMERICA ENTERPRISES

CHAIRMAN & CEO Gary Green
PRESIDENT Larry Botel
GENERAL COUNSEL Matthew Pace
DIRECTOR OF MARKETING Amy Heart
INVESTOR RELATIONS Michele Balfour
DIRECTOR OF OPERATIONS Joan Disalvo
PARTNERS Jon Ashley
Stephen Alepa
Martie Cordaro
Brian Rothschild
Andrew Fox
Ian Ritchie
Dan Waldman
Sonny Kalsi
Glenn Isaacson
Robert Hernreich
Craig Amazeen
Peter Ruprecht
Beryl Snyder
Tom Steiglehner

3STEP

MANAGING PARTNER David Geaslen
CHIEF CONTENT OFFICER Jonathan Segal
CHIEF FINANCIAL OFFICER Sue Murphy

BASEBALL AMERICA(ISSN 0745-5372/USPS 591-210) August 6, 2019, Vol. 39, No. 8 is published monthly, 12 issues per year, by Baseball America Enterprises, LLC, 4319 South Alston Ave, Suite 103, Durham, NC 27713. Subscription rate is $92.95 for one year; Canada $118.95 (U.S. funds); all other foreign $144.95 per year (U.S. funds). Periodicals postage paid at Durham, NC, & additional mailing offices. Occasionally our subscriber list is made available to reputable firms offering goods and services we believe would be of interest to our readers. If you prefer to be excluded, please send your current address label and a note requesting to be excluded from these promotions to Baseball America Enterprises, LLC, 4319 South Alston Ave, Suite 103, Durham, NC 27713, Attn: Privacy Coordinator. POSTMASTER: Send all UAA to CFS (See DMM 707.4.12.5); NON-POSTAL & MILITARY FACILITIES: send address corrections to Baseball America, P.O. Box 420235, Palm Coast, FL 32142-0235. CANADA POST: Return undeliverable Canadian addresses to IMEX Global Solutions, P.O. Box 25542, London, ON N6C 6B2. Please contact 1-800-381-1288 to start carrying Baseball America in your store.
©2019 by Baseball America Enterprises, LLC. All Rights Reserved. Printed in the USA.

BASEBALL AMERICA PRESENTS

BEFORE THEY WERE STARS

SECOND EDITION

Editors
Matt Eddy, Kegan Lowe and J.J. Cooper

Contributing Editors
Chris Hilburn-Trenkle, Michael Magnuson

Database and Application Development
Brent Lewis

Design & Production
Linwood Webb, James Alworth

Programming & Technical Development
Brent Lewis

Cover Photos
MAIN PHOTOS: Ken Griffey Jr. at Angel Stadium in Anahiem, Calif. on May 31, 2009 and Vladimir Guerrero at Angel Stadium on Monday, April 23, 2007. Photos by Jeff Gross/Getty Images and Kirby Lee/Getty Images.

INSET: Ken Griffey Jr. looks on against the Baltimore Orioles at Memorial Stadium in Baltimore, Maryland circa 1989. Photo by Rob Tringali/Sportschrome via Getty Images.

For additional copies, visit our Website at BaseballAmerica.com or call 1-800-845-2726 to order.

US $24.95 / CAN $34.95, plus shipping and handling per order. Expedited shipping available.

Distributed by Simon & Schuster.
ISBN-13: 978-1-932391-91-6

Statistics provided by Major League Baseball Advanced Media and Compiled by Baseball America.

ABOUT THE BOOK

In 2019, the Blue Jays at times fielded a lineup that began with Bo Bichette (son of four-time All-Star Dante Bichette), Cavan Biggio (son of Hall of Famer Craig Biggio) and Vladimir Guerrero Jr. (son of Hall of Famer Vladimir Guerrero). What's remarkable is that by the time they stepped on Toronto's field for the first time, Guerrero and Bichette were arguably the most famous players in Toronto's lineup. Nowadays, top prospects are famous as minor leaguers, and sometimes even as amateurs.

But that wasn't always the case. Besides the occasional spring training sighting, prospects existed in the often-forgotten world of the minor leagues. There were the major leagues, where big league players starred, and the minors, where everyone else worked in obscurity.

Baseball America founder Allan Simpson wanted to change that world. It was his idea to cover the minors (and amateur baseball and the draft) with a focus on picking out the stars of tomorrow long before they arrived. And so he began Baseball America magazine in 1981.

He was crazy to even try. There were no cell phones. The Internet as we know it didn't exist. Statistics came by mail every couple of weeks. Tracking down a scout or front office official meant leaving a long-distance message through voicemail and waiting—hoping—for a callback.

But he and a small group of fellow trailblazers proved that it could be done. From day one, Baseball America ranked prospects, writing scouting reports to provide insights into an area that had previously gone almost unnoticed.

And by doing so, Baseball America helped birth the world we live in today. The one where we all count the days until the next great prospect reaches the majors. Nowadays, it's a given that it's possible to spot future stars before they reach the majors. But that wasn't always the case. It took years of Simpson and his staff being proven right more often than not to get us to this point.

In those early years, many scouts and behind-the-scenes front office officials were excited that someone was paying attention. Some teams simply read their scouting reports over the phone to Simpson to help him prepare Top 10 Prospects rankings. Athletics general manager Sandy Alderson famously relied on Baseball America's Yankees Top 10 Prospects list for his 1985 Rickey Henderson trade—he just asked for the top five Yankees prospects in return.

This book is the fruit of the labor of many scouts and many reporters. Baseball America has worked for nearly 40 years to find tomorrow's stars today. Predicting prospects is extremely difficult and we've had our misses as well as our hits. But this book gives you a chance to see what was expected of the best in baseball before they were household names. Travel back to when they were simply another young player with the dream of becoming a big leaguer, before they were stars.

JJ COOPER
EXECUTIVE EDITOR, BASEBALL AMERICA

ABBREVIATIONS

ABB	LEAGUE	LEVEL
AA	American Association	Triple-A (through 1997)
IL	International	Triple-A
PCL	Pacific Coast	Triple-A
EL	Eastern	Double-A
SL	Southern	Double-A
TL	Texas	Double-A
CAL	California	High Class A
CAR	Carolina	High Class A
FSL	Florida State	High Class A

ABB	LEAGUE	LEVEL
MWL	Midwest	Low Class A
SAL	South Atlantic	Low Class A
NYP	New York-Penn	Short-season
NWL	Northwest	Short-season
APP	Appalachian	Rookie
AZL	Arizona	Rookie
GCL	Gulf Coast	Rookie
PIO	Pioneer	Rookie

A HISTORY OF BASEBALL AMERICA PROSPECT RANKINGS

A few hundred minor league prospects have matured into major league stars in the 39 years that Baseball America has been ranking prospects as comprehensively as only BA can.

Prospect rankings have been an integral part of BA from the beginning in 1981. The October issue from that year ranks the Top 10 Prospects for all of the full-season minor leagues.

The first scouting report to appear in that issue belongs to 20-year-old Phillies shortstop Julio Franco, whose age has since been revised upward by two years. Franco ranked No. 1 in the Eastern League in 1981 and was considered a "can't-miss player who someday soon will replace Larry Bowa in Philadelphia."

Among the other prospects we highlighted in that 1981 issue are current major league managers Terry Francona and Don Mattingly and current broadcasters Ron Darling and Harold Reynolds.

BA began ranking the Top 10 Prospects for each organization beginning with the 1983 season. The National League West was the first division to be featured, and future big leaguers such as Eric Davis, Ozzie Guillen, Kevin McReynolds and Mitch Williams all received reports in that issue.

Best Tools balloting was the next major prospect enhancement. It first appeared on the minor league side in 1983, when minor league managers singled out Dwight Gooden, Orel Hershiser and Kirby Puckett as having loud tools that would impact the game.

The final prospect ranking breakthrough came in the form of the Top 100 Prospects, which was introduced in 1990 and was headlined that year by Steve Avery, Ben McDonald and John Olerud in the top three spots.

ABOUT THE PLAYER SELECTION PROCESS

Filling out the player roster for Before They Were Stars was a daunting task. Because so many minor leaguers have developed into major stars in Baseball America's nearly four decades in the prospect ranking game, I'm still not convinced I chose all the correct players to highlight in this book.

In other words, the player you are convinced got snubbed probably was considered for this book at some point.

When choosing players, I placed an emphasis on peak contributions and concentrated value, such as MVP or Cy Young Award-type seasons, All-Star Game appearances, Gold Gloves won and even Hall of Fame balloting results.

This book was never intended to capture the top 120-plus players of the past 40 years as ranked by an advanced metric such as wins above replacement. Rather, I chose to celebrate big seasons by big stars for whom BA had detailed scouting information dating back to, well, before they were stars.

That last clause disqualified a trio of rookies from the early 1980s who went on to build Hall of Fame careers. Tony Gwynn, Cal Ripken Jr. and Ryne Sandberg all appeared in the pages of BA before they established themselves in the majors, but true scouting information on the trio is scarce.

Fortunately, we had no shortage of worthy candidates to complete our roster, including 22 Hall of Famers for who you might have first received notice in the pages of Baseball America.

MATT EDDY
EXECUTIVE EDITOR, BASEBALL AMERICA

TABLE OF CONTENTS

ABOVE: Bryce Harper. Page 100

ABOVE: Jose Altuve. Page 16

ALL-STAR (AS) • GOLD GLOVE (GG) • MOST VALUABLE PLAYER (MVP) • CY YOUNG AWARD (CYA) • HALL OF FAME (HOF).

PLAYER	POS	SIGNED	PAGE	AWARDS & HONORS				
				AS	GG	MVP	CYA	HOF
Miguel Cabrera	1B	1999	54	11		2		
Robinson Cano	2B	2001	56	8	2			
Chris Carpenter	SP	1993	58	3			1	
Roger Clemens	SP	1983	60	11		1	7	
Gerrit Cole	SP	2011	62	3				
Bartolo Colon	SP	1993	64	4			1	
David Cone	SP	1981	66	5			1	
Johnny Cueto	SP	2004	68	2				
Jacob deGrom	SP	2010	70	3			1	
Carlos Delgado	1B	1988	72	2				
Freddie Freeman	1B	2007	74	4	1			
Eric Gagne	RP	1995	76	3			1	
Nomar Garciaparra	SS	1994	78	6				
Jason Giambi	1B	1992	80	5		1		
Tom Glavine	SP	1984	82	10			2	★
Paul Goldschmidt	1B	2009	84	6	3			
Juan Gonzalez	RF	1986	86	3		2		
Dwight Gooden	SP	1982	88	4			1	
Zack Greinke	SP	2002	90	6	5		1	
Ken Griffey Jr.	CF	1987	92	13	10	1		★
Vladimir Guerrero	RF	1993	94	9		1		★
Roy Halladay	SP	1995	96	8			2	★
Cole Hamels	SP	2002	98	4				
Bryce Harper	RF	2010	100	6		1		
Felix Hernandez	SP	2002	102	6			1	
Trevor Hoffman	RP	1989	104	7				★
Tim Hudson	SP	1997	106	4				
Derek Jeter	SS	1992	108	14	5			
Randy Johnson	SP	1985	110	10			5	★
Andruw Jones	CF	1993	112	5	10			
Chipper Jones	3B	1990	114	8		1		★
Jeff Kent	2B	1989	116	5		1		
Clayton Kershaw	SP	2006	118	8	1	1	3	
Dallas Keuchel	SP	2009	120	2	4		1	
Craig Kimbrel	RP	2008	122	7				
Corey Kluber	SP	2007	124	3			2	
Barry Larkin	SS	1985	126	12	3	1		★
Cliff Lee	SP	2000	128	4			1	
Jon Lester	SP	2002	130	5				
Tim Lincecum	SP	2006	132	4			2	
Francisco Lindor	SS	2011	134	4	1			
Kenny Lofton	CF	1988	136	6	4			
Evan Longoria	3B	2006	138	3	3			
Manny Machado	3B	2010	140	4	2			
Greg Maddux	SP	1984	142	8	18		4	★
Russell Martin	C	2002	144	4	1			
Edgar Martinez	DH	1982	146	7				★
Pedro Martinez	SP	1988	148	8			3	★
Don Mattingly	1B	1979	150	6	9	1		
Joe Mauer	C	2001	152	6	3	1		
Brian McCann	C	2002	154	7				
Andrew McCutchen	CF	2005	156	5	1	1		
Jack McDowell	SP	1987	158	3			1	
Fred McGriff	1B	1981	160	5				
Mark McGwire	1B	1984	162	12	1			

ABOVE: Adrian Beltre. Page 34

BELOW: Francisco Lindor. Page 134

The 2019 Gold Glove, MVP and Cy Young Award winners had not been announced when we went to press.

TABLE OF CONTENTS

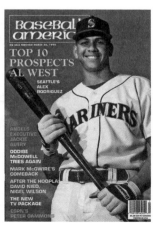

ABOVE: Mike Trout. Page 240

LEFT: Albert Pujols. Page 188

RIGHT: Alex Rodriguez. Page 194

ALL-STAR (AS) · GOLD GLOVE (GG) · MOST VALUABLE PLAYER (MVP) · CY YOUNG AWARD (CYA) · HALL OF FAME (HOF).

PLAYER	POS	SIGNED	PAGE	AWARDS & HONORS				
				AS	GG	MVP	CYA	HOF
Yadier Molina	C	2000	164	9	9			
Mike Mussina	SP	1990	166	5	7			⚫
David Ortiz	DH	1992	168	10				
Roy Oswalt	SP	1997	170	3				
Jake Peavy	SP	1999	172	3	1		1	
Dustin Pedroia	2B	2004	174	4	4	1		
Andy Pettitte	SP	1991	176	3				
Mike Piazza	C	1988	178	12				⚫
Jorge Posada	C	1991	180	5				
Buster Posey	C	2008	182	6	1	1		
David Price	SP	2007	184	5			1	
Kirby Puckett	CF	1982	186	10	6			⚫
Albert Pujols	1B	1999	188	10	2	3		
Manny Ramirez	LF	1991	190	12				
Mariano Rivera	RP	1990	192	13				⚫
Alex Rodriguez	SS	1993	194	14	2	3		
Francisco Rodriguez	RP	1998	196	6				
Ivan Rodriguez	C	1988	198	14	13	1		⚫
Scott Rolen	3B	1993	200	7	8			
Jimmy Rollins	SS	1996	202	3	4	1		
CC Sabathia	SP	1998	204	6			1	
Bret Saberhagen	SP	1982	206	3	1		2	
Chris Sale	SP	2010	208	7				
Johan Santana	SP	1995	210	4	1		2	
Max Scherzer	SP	2006	212	7			3	
Curt Schilling	SP	1986	214	6				
Gary Sheffield	RF	1986	216	9				
John Smoltz	SP	1985	218	8			1	⚫
Blake Snell	SP	2011	220	1			1	
Sammy Sosa	RF	1985	222	7		1		
Giancarlo Stanton	RF	2007	224	4		1		
Stephen Strasburg	SP	2009	226	3				
Darryl Strawberry	RF	1980	228	8				
Ichiro Suzuki	RF	2000	230	10	10	1		
Mark Teixeira	1B	2001	232	3	5			
Miguel Tejada	SS	1993	234	6		1		
Frank Thomas	1B	1989	236	5		2		⚫
Jim Thome	1B	1989	238	5				⚫
Mike Trout	CF	2009	240	8		2		
Troy Tulowitzki	SS	2005	242	5	2			
Chase Utley	2B	2000	244	6				
Robin Ventura	3B	1988	246	2	6			
Justin Verlander	SP	2004	248	8		1	1	
Omar Vizquel	SS	1984	250	3	11			
Joey Votto	1B	2002	252	6	1	1		
Billy Wagner	RP	1993	254	7				
Adam Wainwright	SP	2000	256	3	2			
Larry Walker	RF	1984	258	5	7	1		
Jered Weaver	SP	2004	260	3				
Brandon Webb	SP	2000	262	3			1	
David Wright	3B	2001	264	7	2			
Christian Yelich	LF	2010	266	2	1	1		
Barry Zito	SP	1999	268	3			1	

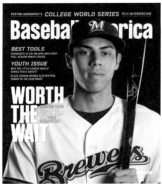

ABOVE: Blake Snell. Page 220

BELOW: Christian Yelich. Page 266

The 2019 Gold Glove, MVP and Cy Young Award winners had not been announced when we went to press.

RONALD ACUÑA JR., OF

BIOGRAPHY

PROPER NAME: Ronald Jose Acuña Jr. **BORN:** December 18, 1997 in La Guaira, Venezuela. **HT:** 6-0. **WT:** 180. **BATS:** R. **THROWS:** R.
FIRST PRO CONTRACT: Signed as international free agent by Braves, July 2, 2014.

2017 MiLB PLAYER OF THE YEAR

ATLANTA BRAVES TOP 10 PROSPECTS FOR 2017

The Braves have been aggressive in challenging Acuna since he signed for a modest $100,000 in 2014. He performed well in his U.S. debut after bypassing the Dominican Summer League in 2015 and proceeded to get off to a fast start at low Class A Rome in 2016 before a broken thumb sidelined him from mid-May to mid-August.

Despite the injury, Acuna displayed his electric tools in all phases of the game. He uses his plus speed to cover center field from gap to gap and has the arm strength to play any position in the garden. He reads balls well, takes good angles and shows impressive anticipation along with excellent first-step quickness. Acuna is aggressive at the plate but has above-average discipline for a teenager.

While his body is still developing, he has plus raw power and barrels pitches consistently with his above-average bat speed. Those traits should allow him to hit for average at higher levels. He needs work on stealing bases more consistently but has the speed to make an impact on the basepaths.

His shortened season at Rome notwithstanding, Acuna should open the 2017 campaign at high Class A Florida after making up for lost time in the winter Australian Baseball League. Though risky, Acuna has as high a ceiling as any Braves position player.

— Bill Ballew

MINOR LEAGUE MENTIONS BY BA

YEAR	TOP 100	ORG RANKING	LEAGUE RANKING	BEST TOOLS
2015			**No. 11:** Gulf Coast **No. 14:** Appalachian	
2016		**No. 26:** Braves	**No. 12:** South Atlantic	
2017	No. 67	**No. 6:** Braves	**No. 1:** Southern **No. 1:** International	**FSL:** Most Exciting Player **SL:** Best Batting Prospect, Most Exciting Player
2018	No. 1	**No. 1:** Braves		**IL:** Best Batting Prospect, Best Power Prospect, Best Defensive OF, Most Exciting Player

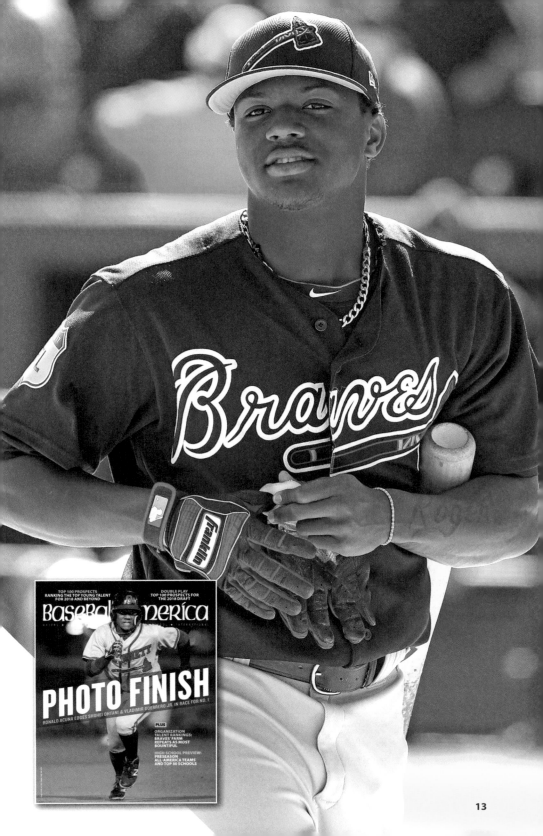

ROBERTO ALOMAR, 2B

BIOGRAPHY

PROPER NAME: Roberto Alomar Velázquez. **BORN:** February 5, 1968 in Ponce, Puerto Rico.
HT: 6-0. **WT:** 185. **BATS:** B. **THROWS:** R. **SCHOOL:** Luis Munoz Rivera HS, Salinas, Puerto Rico.
FIRST PRO CONTRACT: Signed as international free agent by Padres, Feb. 16, 1985.

SAN DIEGO PADRES TOP 10 PROSPECTS FOR 1986

The son of former major-league infielder Sandy Alomar, Roberto Alomar began his pro career last season as the youngest player in the South Atlantic League but hardly was overwhelmed (.293, 54 RBIs, 36 SB).

All but 17 of his 160 hits were singles, but scouts like his offensive potential. As he grows stronger, his speed will make him an extra-base hitter. And with instruction, he eventually may steal 55-60 bases a year.

Although he made 36 errors as a second baseman last season, Alomar is a gifted defender. He has terrific hands and the range of a shortstop, which might be his position. The arm is strong, but sometimes erratic.

Roberto and his older brother by a year, Sandy Jr., played at Charleston last season, and their father was a coach. Sandy Jr. is a good catching prospect, although scouts doubt that he'll hit.

— **Ken Leiker**

TEXAS LEAGUE TOP 10 PROSPECTS FOR 1987

One manager said Alomar may not get to the majors until 1991, "but he's just going to get better and better."

Alomar converted from second base to shortstop this year. The consensus: He's not there yet, but he'll be great in a few years.

"If he was a second baseman, I could see him play in the big leagues next year," Wichita manager Steve Smith said. "In one year he's really developed into a shortstop. It seems like the tougher the pitcher the better he hits him."

— **Mike Knobler**

MINOR LEAGUE MENTIONS BY BA

YEAR	TOP 100	ORG RANKING	LEAGUE RANKING	BEST TOOLS
1986		**No. 4:** Padres	**No. 3:** California	
1987		**No. 4:** Padres	**No. 8:** Texas	**TL:** Best Defensive SS
1988		**No. 1:** Padres		

Baseball
america

ON SALE THROUGH NOVEMBER 26, 1992

SECOND
TO NONE

TORONTO'S
ROBERTO ALOMAR,
CREAM OF THE
FREE-AGENT CROP

AL DRAFT
REPORT CARDS

THE PRESSURE ON
FIRST-ROUND PICKS

BASEBALL FEVER
GRIPS SEATTLE

TONY GWYNN
AT THE MOVIES

JOSE ALTUVE, 2B

BIOGRAPHY

PROPER NAME: Jose Carlos Altuve. **BORN:** May 6, 1990 in Maracay, Venezuela.
HT: 5-6. **WT:** 165. **BATS:** R. **THROWS:** R.
FIRST PRO CONTRACT: Signed as international free agent by Astros, March 6, 2007.

HOUSTON ASTROS TOP 30 PROSPECTS FOR 2012

Altuve fits no standard profile. He doesn't lack tools, but he's difficult to compare to other players. He has a unique build, compared by some scouts to a fire hydrant, and some say he is two inches shorter than his listed height. At the end of last season, he may have been 10 pounds lighter as well. But he has baseball skills and enough tools to make things interesting.

Defense is his best attribute. He has quick, strong hands that work well at the plate and in the field. He's agile and at times a dazzling second baseman, with arm strength to turn the double play well. He has developed a good rapport with shortstop Jio Mier, whom he has played with the last two seasons, and has gotten in time at third base as well.

Offensively, Altuve shows enough power to punish mistakes but mostly plays a No. 2 hitter's game. He uses the whole field, has excellent baserunning skills that augment his average speed and shows the bat control to move runners. Altuve plays with energy that makes him a team leader and keeps winning people over.

He may put up big numbers at Lancaster this season but will have to keep proving himself at higher levels to scouts who remain skeptical of a player with such a small body

— **John Manuel**

MINOR LEAGUE MENTIONS BY BA

YEAR	TOP 100	ORG RANKING	LEAGUE RANKING	BEST TOOLS
2010				**SAL:** Best Defensive 2B
2011		**No. 28:** Astros	**No. 15:** California	

NOLAN ARENADO, 3B

BIOGRAPHY

PROPER NAME: Nolan James Arenado. **BORN:** April 16, 1991 in Lake Forest, Calif.
HT: 6-2. **WT:** 205. **BATS:** R. **THROWS:** R. **SCHOOL:** El Toro HS, Lake Forest, Calif.
FIRST PRO CONTRACT: Selected by Rockies in second round (59th overall) of 2009 draft;
signed July 7, 2009.

COLORADO ROCKIES TOP 10 PROSPECTS FOR 2012

After missing the first six weeks in 2010 with a groin injury, Arenado broke out in 2011, leading the minors with 122 RBIs and flourishing in the Arizona Fall League. He won AFL MVP honors after batting .388 and leading the league in hits (47), doubles (12) and extra-base hits (18). He also improved on defense, ending talk that his range and first-step quickness would prompt a move from third to first base.

Arenado has exceptional hand-eye coordination and very quick, strong hands. He entered pro ball with an advanced two-strike approach and has learned to turn on pitches when he gets the opportunity. His swing has a flat path, but he gets good extension and has shown an increased ability to hit balls with backspin, which should lead to solid or better power. He controls the strike zone well and is starting to draw more walks.

Arenado dropped 20 pounds last offseason, resulting in average range at third base despite his lack of quick feet. He has soft hands and plenty of arm strength, with plus accuracy and a quick release from any angle. He's a well below-average runner.

Arenado has the work ethic to maintain his defensive skills. He's competitive but can show his youth by getting emotional at times. A potential No. 3 hitter, Arenado should open 2012 in Double-A, with a second-half promotion to the big leagues a possibility. He could be ready for a regular role in Colorado by 2013.

— Jack Etkin

MINOR LEAGUE MENTIONS BY BA

YEAR	TOP 100	ORG RANKING	LEAGUE RANKING	BEST TOOLS
2009			**No. 8:** Pioneer	
2010		**No. 10:** Rockies	**No. 2:** South Atlantic	
2011	No. 80	**No. 3:** Rockies	**No. 6:** California	**CAL:** Best Defensive 3B
2012	No. 42	**No. 2:** Rockies	**No. 8:** Texas	**TL:** Best Defensive 3B
2013	No. 52	**No. 1:** Rockies		

JAKE ARRIETA, RHP

BIOGRAPHY

PROPER NAME: Jacob Joseph Arrieta. **BORN:** March 6, 1986 in Farmington, Mo.
HT: 6-4. **WT:** 225. **BATS:** R. **THROWS:** R. **SCHOOL:** Texas Christian.
FIRST PRO CONTRACT: Selected by Orioles in fifth round (159th overall) of 2007 draft;
signed Aug. 15, 2007.

BALTIMORE ORIOLES TOP 10 PROSPECTS FOR 2009

Though he didn't perform well as a college junior, Arrieta had shown first-round stuff during his amateur career, so the Orioles gave him $1.1 million as a fifth-round pick in the 2007 draft. He looked well worth it in his 2008 pro debut, finishing as the Carolina League's ERA leader, pitcher of the year and top pitching prospect despite dealing with an oblique injury in June and departing early to pitch for the U.S. Olympic team. He made one start in Beijing, pitching six shutout innings with seven strikeouts against China.

The Orioles thought Arrieta could get his velocity back with minor mechanical adjustments, and they were right. His fastball peaked at 96-97 mph in 2008 and showed explosive late movement, and he got stronger with more work. He shows good fastball command and isn't afraid to pitch inside, and his big frame should allow him to eat innings.

Arrieta could have as many as three plus pitches to go with his fastball, but they all need work. His slider has the most potential, but his changeup should also be a good pitch as he uses it more. His curveball is a slow, big breaker that he'll need to tighten up.

Some observers believe Arrieta will be better than both Chris Tillman and Brian Matusz, and the Orioles will be happy if they can build their future rotation.

— **Will Lingo**

MINOR LEAGUE MENTIONS BY BA

YEAR	TOP 100	ORG RANKING	LEAGUE RANKING	BEST TOOLS
2008		**No. 7:** Orioles	**No. 2:** Carolina	**CAR:** Best Fastball
2009	No. 67	**No. 4:** Orioles	**No. 17:** Eastern **No. 11:** International	
2010	No. 99	**No. 4:** Orioles	**No. 14:** International	

JAVIER BAEZ, SS

BIOGRAPHY

PROPER NAME: Ednel Javier Baez. **BORN:** December 1, 1992 in Toa Baja, Puerto Rico.
HT: 6-0. **WT:** 190. **BATS:** R. **THROWS:** R. **SCHOOL:** Arlington Country Day HS, Jacksonville.
FIRST PRO CONTRACT: Selected by Cubs in first round (ninth overall) of 2011 draft;
signed Aug. 15, 2011.

CHICAGO CUBS TOP 10 PROSPECTS FOR 2012

Born in Puerto Rico, Baez moved to Florida in 2005 and batted .711 with 20 homers as a high school senior last spring. Though the Cubs need pitching, they passed on several college arms to draft him ninth overall last June. He signed for $2.625 million at the Aug. 15 deadline.

Baez had the best bat speed in the 2011 draft, prompting comparisons to Gary Sheffield and Hanley Ramirez. In terms of the 20-80 scouting scale, Chicago thinks Baez could develop into a 70 hitter with 65 power. He's still learning that he doesn't have to overswing to do damage. His arm strength gives him a third well above-average tool and may allow him to stay at shortstop.

Baez is an average runner with average range who will have to find a new position if he loses a step, with third base perhaps the best long-term fit. Second base, right field and even catcher are other options. Overly aggressive and emotional at times, he'll need time to mature on and off the field.

Baez has the highest ceiling in the system and could move quickly. His bat eventually should fit into the No. 3 slot in Chicago's lineup and should provide enough offense for any position. He'll head to low Class A Peoria at age 19.

— Jim Callis

MINOR LEAGUE MENTIONS BY BA

YEAR	TOP 100	ORG RANKING	LEAGUE RANKING	BEST TOOLS
2012	No. 61	**No. 2:** Cubs	**No. 1:** Midwest	**MWL:** Most Exciting Player
2013	No. 16	**No. 1:** Cubs	**No. 3:** Florida State **No. 3:** Southern	**FSL:** Best INF Arm
2014	No. 5	**No. 1:** Cubs	**No. 3:** Pacific Coast	**PCL:** Best Power Prospect, Best INF Arm

JEFF BAGWELL, 1B

BIOGRAPHY

PROPER NAME: Jeffrey Robert Bagwell. **BORN:** May 27, 1968 in Boston, Mass.
HT: 6-0. **WT:** 195. **BATS:** R. **THROWS:** R. **SCHOOL:** Hartford.
FIRST PRO CONTRACT: Selected by Red Sox in fourth round (110th overall) of 1989 draft;
signed June 10, 1989.

EASTERN LEAGUE TOP 10 PROSPECTS FOR 1990

Bagwell's numbers were staggering in his first professional season. He finished second in hitting, playing half his games at Beehive Field, one of the toughest parks for hitters in the minors. Bagwell broke the New Britain season record for hits, led the league in hits and doubles, and was second in triples.

Said Canton manager Ken Bolek: "He's proved day in, day out that he's the best hitter in the league. And the amazing thing is that he's been steady all year. This is his first full year, and he's proved himself in a very difficult league."

In a move to shore up their bullpen, the Red Sox traded Bagwell to the Astros for reliever Larry Andersen.

— **Phil Bowman**

HOUSTON ASTROS TOP 10 PROSPECTS FOR 1991

Boston's decision to trade Bagwell to Houston after the minor league season was not a popular one in New England. Bagwell was a University of Hartford product, one of New England's own.

Bagwell missed winning the Eastern League batting title by one point in 1990, a significant feat for a below-average runner. He's got an excellent stroke, takes pitches well, makes contact and uses the whole park.

Bagwell is not Ken Caminiti at third base, though he has a chance to inherit his job this spring if Caminiti is dealt for much-needed pitching. He does not have Caminiti's superb arm but is considered an above-average thrower.

— **Allan Simpson**

MINOR LEAGUE MENTIONS BY BA

YEAR	TOP 100	ORG RANKING	LEAGUE RANKING	BEST TOOLS
1990			**No. 4:** Eastern	**EL:** Best Hitter
1991	No. 32	**No. 2:** Astros		

JOSH BECKETT, RHP

2001 MiLB PLAYER OF THE YEAR

BIOGRAPHY

PROPER NAME: Josh Patrick Beckett. **BORN:** May 15, 1980 in Spring, Texas.
HT: 6-5. **WT:** 230. **BATS:** R. **THROWS:** R. **SCHOOL:** Spring (Texas) HS.
FIRST PRO CONTRACT: Selected by Marlins in first round (second overall)
of 1999 draft; signed Sept. 1, 1999.

FLORIDA MARLINS TOP 10 PROSPECTS FOR 2000

BACKGROUND: Beckett was drafted No. 2 overall in June, becoming the first high school righthander since Bill Gullickson (1979) to be taken that high. He signed a four-year, $7 million major league contract just days before he was to head to Blinn (Texas) Junior College.

STRENGTHS: Beckett is the same age as many college sophomores. He has a prototypical power pitcher's build and has been clocked as high as 97 mph, though he topped out at 94 during instructional league. He has a devastating 12-to-6 curveball that breaks hard and late. Though extremely confident, Beckett is coachable and willing to learn.

WEAKNESSES: Beckett is inexperienced and needs to work on finishing his pitches. His changeup is still developing, but the arm speed and command are there already.

FUTURE: He will begin 2000 at either low Class A Kane County or at high Class A Brevard County. All indications point to a rapid pass through the Marlins' system.

— Mike Berardino

MINOR LEAGUE MENTIONS BY BA

YEAR	TOP 100	ORG RANKING	LEAGUE RANKING	BEST TOOLS
2000	No. 19	**No. 2:** Marlins	**No. 1:** Midwest	**MWL:** Best Fastball
2001	No. 3	**No. 1:** Marlins	**No. 1:** Florida State **No. 1:** Eastern	**FSL:** Best Pitching Prospect, Best Fastball, Best Breaking Pitch **EL:** Best Pitching Prospect
2002	No. 1	**No. 1:** Marlins		

ALBERT BELLE, OF

BIOGRAPHY

PROPER NAME: Albert Jojuan Belle. **BORN:** August 25, 1966 in Shreveport, La.
HT: 6-2. **WT:** 210. **BATS:** R. **THROWS:** R. **SCHOOL:** Louisiana State.
FIRST PRO CONTRACT: Selected by Indians in second round (47th overall) of 1987 draft;
signed Aug. 27, 1987.

CLEVELAND INDIANS TOP 10 PROSPECTS FOR 1988

A second-round pick out of Louisiana State (the Indians lost their No. 1 selection for signing Rick Dempsey, of all people), Belle has the best pure talent in the organization. In fact, many scouts say based on talent he might have been the best player available in last June's draft.

The problem is, attitude is a big part of this game, and Belle has to learn to control his emotions if he's ever going to make the most of his ability. Things got so out of hand at LSU last year that he was thrown off the team and didn't even go to the College World Series.

There also was a flareup in the Florida Instructional League, but Belle was back, after apologizing for his actions, the next day. He can run, throw and hit for average as well as power.

— **Tracy Ringolsby**

EASTERN LEAGUE TOP 10 PROSPECTS FOR 1989

Heading into 1989, nobody ever questioned Belle's talent, only his attitude. The Indians organization suspended him twice in 1988. But in 1989, he was more Gentleman Joey than Bad Boy Belle.

Belle was hitting .282 with 20 home runs and 69 RBIs when he went to the majors. He hit 12 of the home runs in a 75 at-bat stretch and was threatening league records for homers and RBIs.

"Incredible tools," Harrisburg manager Dave Trembly said. "He can hit the ball out of the park, and he can run the bases. He's a decent outfielder, too. Now that he's reached the majors, I think he will play with a little more excitement."

— **Phil Bowman**

| **MINOR LEAGUE MENTIONS BY BA** | | | | |
YEAR	TOP 100	ORG RANKING	LEAGUE RANKING	BEST TOOLS
1988		**No. 6:** Indians		
1989		**No. 3:** Indians	**No. 1:** Eastern	**EL:** Best Hitter, Best Power

CODY BELLINGER, OF

PROPER NAME: Cody James Bellinger. **BORN:** July 13, 1995 in Scottsdale, Ariz.
HT: 6-4. **WT:** 203. **BATS:** L. **THROWS:** L. **SCHOOL:** Hamilton HS, Chandler, Ariz.
FIRST PRO CONTRACT: Selected by Dodgers in fourth round (124th overall) of 2013 draft;
signed June 13, 2013.

LOS ANGELES DODGERS TOP 10 PROSPECTS FOR 2016

Bellinger entered pro ball with a high baseball IQ because his father, Clay, played four seasons in the majors. In 2015, the Dodgers aggressively jumped Bellinger to high Class A Rancho Cucamonga, where he transformed from a sweet swinger into a 30-home run hitter.

He used to gear his swing for line drives, but he made an adjustment in 2015 to create torque. He started loading his hands rather than using more of his body in his swing, allowing him to get closer to his launch position and use his hands to drive the ball.

That helped his plus power show up in games, with quick bat speed, good leverage and use of his lower half. The changes contributed to a 28 percent strikeout rate. Near the end of 2015, he studied heat maps to understand his strengths and weaknesses. Thus, his strikeout rate dropped to 19 percent in August.

Bellinger is an exceptional athlete for a first baseman, a smooth, above-average defender with quick feet and a strong arm. He's a solid-average runner, which is why he played in center field for 21 games. He'll open 2016 as a 20-year-old at Double-A Tulsa. If he can find the right blend of contact and power, he can be an above-average regular at first.

— **Ben Badler**

MINOR LEAGUE MENTIONS BY BA

YEAR	TOP 100	ORG RANKING	LEAGUE RANKING	BEST TOOLS
2014		**No. 14:** Dodgers	**No. 10:** Pioneer	
2015		**No. 20:** Dodgers	**No. 13:** California	**CAL:** Best Defensive 1B
2016	No. 54	**No. 5:** Dodgers	**No. 2:** Texas	**TL:** Best Defensive 1B
2017	No. 7	**No. 1:** Dodgers		

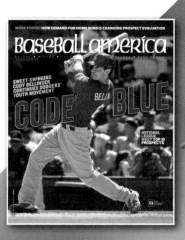

CARLOS BELTRAN, OF

BIOGRAPHY

PROPER NAME: Carlos Ivan Beltran. **BORN:** April 24, 1977 in Manati, Puerto Rico.
HT: 6-1. **WT:** 215. **BATS:** B. **THROWS:** R. **SCHOOL:** Fernando Callejo HS, Manati, Puerto Rico.
FIRST PRO CONTRACT: Selected by Royals in second round (49th overall) of the 1995 draft;
signed June 5, 1995.

KANSAS CITY ROYALS TOP 10 PROSPECTS FOR 1997

BACKGROUND: The Royals were divided on whether to draft Beltran or Juan LeBron with their first-round pick in 1995. They took LeBron, but Beltran has quickly become the more favored prospect.

STRENGTHS: Beltran is a five-tool player. He's a natural center fielder with above-average speed and an exceptional arm. He has such uncanny hitting instincts that he took to switch-hitting in 1996 almost overnight.

WEAKNESSES: Beltran gets overanxious trying to hit the ball out of the park. He needs to refine his bunting ability to take advantage of his speed.

FUTURE: Nagging injuries and cold weather hurt Beltran's performance at Class A Lansing, but he could skip that step with a strong performance this winter in Puerto Rico.

— **Allan Simpson**

TEXAS LEAGUE TOP 10 PROSPECTS FOR 1998

Beltran didn't come to the league until July, but he quickly made an impact.

Like other five-tooled outfielders, Beltran flashed a nice arm, good speed and a quick, powerful bat. He made the transition from Class A look simple.

"It was real easy for him," Wichita manager John Mizerock said. "He has the physical tools to be a superstar."

— **George Schroeder**

MINOR LEAGUE MENTIONS BY BA

YEAR	TOP 100	ORG RANKING	LEAGUE RANKING	BEST TOOLS
1995			**No. 9:** Gulf Coast	
1996		**No. 4:** Royals	**No. 8:** Northwest	
1997	No. 93	**No. 2:** Royals		**CAR:** Best Defensive OF
1998		**No. 5:** Royals	**No. 7:** Carolina **No. 5:** Texas	**CAR:** Best Defensive OF, Best OF Arm, Most Exciting Player
1999	No. 14	**No 1:** Royals		

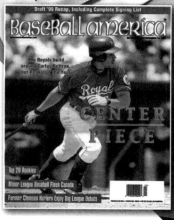

Draft '99 Recap, Including Complete Signing List

Baseball america

The Royals build
around Carlos Beltran,
our Rookie of the Year.

CENTER
PIECE

Top 20 Rookies

Minor League Baseball Flees Canada

Former Clemson Hurlers Enjoy Big League Debuts

ADRIAN BELTRE, 3B

BIOGRAPHY

PROPER NAME: Adrian Beltre Perez.
BORN: April 7, 1979 in Santo Domingo, Dominican Republic.
HT: 5-11. **WT:** 220. **BATS:** R. **THROWS:** R.
SCHOOL: Liceo Maximo Gomez, Santo Domingo, Dominican Republic.
FIRST PRO CONTRACT: Signed as international free agent by Dodgers, July 7, 1994.

SOUTH ATLANTIC LEAGUE TOP 10 PROSPECTS FOR 1996

Prospect watchers came for the offense and stayed for the defense. Beltre showed four tools and projects as an improved runner. Managers loved Beltre's aggressiveness at the plate and rated his arm as the best among SAL infielders.

"Adrian adjusted as if he had been playing professionally for years," Savannah manager John Shoemaker said. "He was ready to hit every pitch thrown to him. Of all the tools he has, his maturity may have been what stood out."

— **Gene Sapakoff**

LOS ANGELES DODGERS TOP 10 PROSPECTS FOR 1997

BACKGROUND: Beltre's first season in the United States was impressive. He was named the top prospect in the South Atlantic League and was ranked No. 9 in the California League, where he was the youngest player.

STRENGTHS: Beltre is a four-tool player with everything except above-average speed. He has an outstanding arm, great hands and hits for average and power. His instincts and physique remind some of [Raúl] Mondesi.

WEAKNESSES: Speed and experience are the only thing missing in Beltre's game. The former isn't a necessity and the latter will come as he progresses.

THE FUTURE: Beltre will probably start the season with Class A Vero Beach. If he has a good first half, he'll move to San Antonio.

— **Gary Klein**

MINOR LEAGUE MENTIONS BY BA

YEAR	TOP 100	ORG RANKING	LEAGUE RANKING	BEST TOOLS
1996			No. 1: South Atlantic No. 9: California	SAL: Best Hitter, Best Power, Best Defensive 3B, Best INF Arm, Most Exciting Player
1997	No. 30	No. 4: Dodgers	No. 1: Florida State	FSL: Best Hitter, Best Power, Best Defensive 3B, Best INF Arm, Most Exciting Player
1998	No. 3	No. 2: Dodgers	No. 1: Texas	TL: Best Hitter, Best Defensive 3B, Best INF Arm, Most Exciting Player

EZRA O. SHAW/ALLSPORT | ISSUE DATE: SEPTEMBER, 2018

MOOKIE BETTS, OF

BIOGRAPHY

PROPER NAME: Markus Lynn Betts. **BORN:** October 7, 1992 in Brentwood, Tenn.
HT: 5-9. **WT:** 180. **BATS:** R. **THROWS:** R. **SCHOOL:** Overton HS, Brentwood, Tenn.
FIRST PRO CONTRACT: Selected by Red Sox in fifth round (172nd overall) of 2011 draft;
signed June 7, 2011.

SOUTH ATLANTIC LEAGUE TOP 10 PROSPECTS FOR 2013

No one was more of a revelation in the South Atlantic League than Betts, a 5-foot-9 second baseman with surprising strength.

"He's one of the better hitters I've seen this year," an NL scout said. "He sees the ball so early and stays inside the ball very well."

A former shortstop, Betts has found a home at second, where he has solid range and good hands. He's an above-average runner, but he's an even better basestealer because he knows how to pick his spots and get good jumps.

— **J.J. Cooper**

INTERNATIONAL LEAGUE TOP 10 PROSPECTS FOR 2014

Betts starred as a second baseman on his way up the minor league ladder, but with Dustin Pedroia locked in at the keystone in Boston, the Red Sox shifted Betts to center field when he reached Pawtucket in mid-June. He adjusted quickly and profiles as at least an average overall defender there.

"Making the adjustment from the infield to the outfield shows what kind of an athlete he is," Pawtucket manager Kevin Boles said. "His ability to hit through the zone to all fields makes him a dangerous hitter, plus he's a threat on the basepaths."

Betts' athleticism, above-average speed and elite on-base skills should make him a perfect fit as Boston's leadoff hitter. He makes the most of his diminutive frame by showing good patience with occasional power. His compact right-handed swing with above-average pitch recognition make him a tough out.

— **Vincent Lara-Cinisomo**

MINOR LEAGUE MENTIONS BY BA

YEAR	TOP 100	ORG RANKING	LEAGUE RANKING	BEST TOOLS
2013		**No. 31:** Red Sox	**No. 8:** South Atlantic **No. 7:** Carolina	**SAL:** Best Strike-Zone Judgment
2014	No. 75	**No. 7:** Red Sox	**No. 2:** Eastern **No. 2:** International	**EL:** Best Defensive 2B

CRAIG BIGGIO, 2B

BIOGRAPHY

PROPER NAME: Craig Alan Biggio. **BORN:** December 14, 1965 in Smithtown, N.Y.
HT: 5-11. **WT:** 185. **BATS:** R. **THROWS:** R. **SCHOOL:** Seton Hall.
FIRST PRO CONTRACT: Selected by Astros in first round (22nd overall) of 1987 draft;
signed June 8, 1987.

SOUTH ATLANTIC LEAGUE TOP 10 PROSPECTS FOR 1987

Managers were in agreement that Biggio, Houston's No. 1 draft pick in June, has all the tools and all the right intangibles to make the major leagues.

The disagreement is where. Few think it will be as a catcher.

"He is definitely the top prospect or among the top two," [Asheville manager Keith] Bodie said. "He probably will play in the big leagues before anyone in this league."

Why? Biggio can hit, hit with power, throw and run. He stole 31 bases, while batting .375, in just 64 games. The opinions on his arm strength varied from good to fair. Managers also raved about his desire and hustle.

— **Richard Chesley**

HOUSTON ASTROS TOP 10 PROSPECTS FOR 1988

The Astros' No. 1 selection last June out of Seton Hall, Biggio has the tools to develop into a solid big league player.

He has power (17 doubles, nine home runs and 49 RBIs in 216 at-bats at Class A Asheville in his taste at pro ball). He has speed (31 stolen bases). And he knows the strike zone (39 walks and 33 strikeouts).

The question, though, is where Biggio will eventually play in the big leagues. For now, the Astros will try to refine him into a decent catcher. He is part of that new breed of one-handed catchers who is going to have to make marked improvement in the quickness with which he moves his free hand. His throwing mechanics also need refining.

— **Tracy Ringolsby**

MINOR LEAGUE MENTIONS BY BA

YEAR	TOP 100	ORG RANKING	LEAGUE RANKING	BEST TOOLS
1987			**No. 4:** South Atlantic	
1988		**No. 1:** Astros		

The New League: Is It A Threat?

Introducing The Catchers Of The '90s

BaseBall america

"Baseball News You Can't Get Anywhere Else"

September 10-24, 1989

Price $1.95 ($2.50 In Canada)

Now In Our 9th Year

CATCH A RISING ASTRO

Craig Biggio Heads A Cast Of Talented Young Catchers

Major League Columnist

Complete Minor League Coverage

Steve Ganer; A Pitching Prospect Starts Over

BARRY BONDS, OF

BIOGRAPHY

PROPER NAME: Barry Lamar Bonds. **BORN:** July 24, 1964 in Riverside, Calif.
HT: 6-2. **WT:** 240. **BATS:** L. **THROWS:** L. **SCHOOL:** Arizona State.
FIRST PRO CONTRACT: Selected by Pirates in first round (sixth overall) of 1985 draft;
signed June 5, 1985.

CAROLINA LEAGUE TOP 10 PROSPECTS FOR 1985

Bonds was the Pirates' No. 1 pick in the June draft and the No. 6 pick over-all. Therefore, he didn't join the the league until mid-June, but Bonds managed to impress just about everyone who saw him.

"He can do it all," Hagerstown manager Greg Biagini said. "He has the quickest bat in the league. His swing has no extra motion in it at all. He can do just about what he wants to. He's fun to watch."

— Bruce Winkworth

PITTSBURGH PIRATES TOP 10 PROSPECTS FOR 1986

The sixth player chosen in last June's draft, there's no question about his talent. On skills alone, he probably would have been the first player taken, but some teams were scared off by what one scout described as "a Mel Hall mentality—talk, talk, talk, me, me, me." The Pirates prefer to call it "a healthy confidence."

Bonds had no trouble adjusting to a wooden bat at Prince William (.299, 13 HR, 37 RBIs, 15 SB), and he also showed more consistent power than he had at Arizona State. His announced goal of following in the footsteps of his father Bobby, as a 30-30 (homers, stolen bases) player in the big leagues may not be out of the question, although he's more of a runner than a basestealer.

He's instinctive in center field and can cover the alleys, but his arm may keep him in left. The early reports on his play in Venezuela this winter were so good the Pirates were beginning to have ideas about him possibly jumping to the varsity in the spring.

— Ken Leiker

MINOR LEAGUE MENTIONS BY BA

YEAR	TOP 100	ORG RANKING	LEAGUE RANKING	BEST TOOLS
1985			No. 3: Carolina	
1986		No. 1: Pirates		

71 sons of ex-big leaguers playing pro ball

The mystique of Cuba's national baseball team

Baseball america

"Baseball News
You Can't Get
Anywhere Else . . ."

September 10-24, 1985
Price: $1.90 ($2.75 in Canada)
Now in our 5th year

**FOLLOWING IN
DAD'S FOOTSTEPS**

DICK YOUNG

PIRATES
51

41

RYAN BRAUN, OF

BIOGRAPHY

PROPER NAME: Ryan Joseph Braun. **BORN:** November 17, 1983 in Mission Hills, Calif.
HT: 6-2. **WT:** 205. **BATS:** R. **THROWS:** R. **SCHOOL:** Miami.
FIRST PRO CONTRACT: Selected by Brewers in first round (fifth overall) of 2005 draft;
signed June 18, 2005.

SOUTH ATLANTIC LEAGUE TOP 10 PROSPECTS FOR 2005

West Virginia got a very young, talented team for its first year of affiliation with the Brewers. Braun, the fifth overall pick in the 2005 draft, was part of a group of second-half reinforcements who helped make the Power respectable. The Brewers hope Braun can join Prince Fielder, Rickie Weeks and J.J. Hardy in their homegrown infield of the future.

While Braun will need repetitions to overcome his inexperience and stiffness at the hot corner, his bat should move him toward Milwaukee quickly. His quick hands generate excellent bat speed, and he whips the bat through the zone with some uppercut and a high finish. His power is his best tool, and he's also a plus runner with above-average arm strength. His footwork and work ethic will determine whether he can stay at third base or will have to move to an outfield corner.

— **Chris Gigley**

FLORIDA STATE LEAGUE TOP 10 PROSPECTS FOR 2006

Braun was the one Florida State League hitter who left scouts and managers with little to question. He showed present power, and with a smooth swing, he also should hit for average.

At third base, he projects as an average defender with solid range and a slightly above-average arm, though his hands and reactions could use some work. On the basepaths, he's an above-average runner.

"He pretty much does everything," Fort Myers manager Kevin Boles said. "He has a chance to be a special player. He does it all."

— **J.J. Cooper**

MINOR LEAGUE MENTIONS BY BA

YEAR	TOP 100	ORG RANKING	LEAGUE RANKING	BEST TOOLS
2005			**No. 5:** South Atlantic	
2006	No. 49	**No. 3:** Brewers	**No. 4:** Florida State **No. 6:** Southern	**FSL:** Best Hitter, Best Defensive 3B
2007	No. 26	**No. 2:** Brewers		**PCL:** Best Hitter, Most Exciting Player

ALEX BREGMAN, 3B

BIOGRAPHY

PROPER NAME: Alexander David Bregman. **BORN:** March 30, 1994 in Albuquerque, N.M.
HT: 6-0. **WT:** 180. **BATS:** R. **THROWS:** R. **SCHOOL:** Louisiana State.
FIRST PRO CONTRACT: Selected by Astros in first round (second overall) of 2015 draft;
signed June 25, 2015.

HOUSTON ASTROS TOP 10 PROSPECTS FOR 2016

Bregman has been one of the best players everywhere he's ever played. A USA Baseball veteran since early in his high school days, he was the BA Freshman of the Year in 2013, a two-time first-team All-American for Louisiana State and, ultimately, the second overall pick in the 2015 draft. His $5.9 million signing bonus ranks second in Astros history.

Blessed with excellent hand-eye coordination and a simple, level swing, Bregman has plenty of bat speed and is equally comfortable yanking the ball down the left-field line or staying back and stinging a ball to the right-field wall. He should be at least a plus hitter who racks up walks as well.

Defensively, Bregman is the kind of player who grows on evaluators the longer they see him. His range is average at best and his arm is only average as well, but he anticipates exceptionally well and plays with a smooth unruffled grace. Nothing surprises him and the ball never seems to eat him up. He's an above-average runner who runs the bases well.

Bregman has the power to hit 10-15 home runs a year at the expense to his average, but he's at his best when he's spraying line drives. He is one of the safer college picks in recent years with a long track record of success and a Carlos Correa-like drive to succeed, but without Correa's physical gifts.

At worst, Bregman should be an everyday second baseman who hits for average with occasional power. He's blocked with the Astros by Correa and second baseman Jose Altuve, but if traded he could be an above-average offensive shortstop with reliable defense. He's on the fast track and should spend much of 2016 at Double-A Corpus Christi.

— **J.J. Cooper**

MINOR LEAGUE MENTIONS BY BA

YEAR	TOP 100	ORG RANKING	LEAGUE RANKING	BEST TOOLS
2015			**No. 5:** California	
2016	No. 42	**No. 3:** Astros	**No. 1:** Texas	**TL:** Best Batting Prospect, Best Strike-Zone Judgment, Best Defensive SS, Most Exciting Player

KEVIN BROWN, RHP

BIOGRAPHY

PROPER NAME: James Kevin Brown. **BORN:** March 14, 1965 in Milledgeville, Ga.
HT: 6-4. **WT:** 195. **BATS:** R. **THROWS:** R. **SCHOOL:** Georgia Tech.
FIRST PRO CONTRACT: Selected by Rangers in first round (fourth overall) of 1986 draft;
singed July 17, 1986.

TEXAS LEAGUE TOP 10 PROSPECTS FOR 1988

After going 1-11 last year and starting this year 2-7, Brown underwent a transformation, regained his confidence and pitched inside.

"He pitched like a major leaguer against us," Jackson manager Tucker Ashford said.

"If he throws strikes, there's no reason he can't pitch in the big leagues today," El Paso manager Dave Machemer said.

— **Mike Knobler**

TEXAS RANGERS TOP 10 PROSPECTS FOR 1989

The Rangers' No. 1 draft pick out of Georgia Tech in 1986 turned looming disaster into the system's best hope during the 1988 season. After winning on Opening Day, 1987, Brown went on a 14-game losing streak, which included his first three decisions of 1988. By early June, he was 2-7 with Tulsa and on the verge of demotion to Class A for the second year in a row.

Bang. Brown found that 95 mph fastball, combined it with his version of a split-finger pitch, and he suddenly matured. He didn't let what he felt was a bad play or a bad call rattle him. And Brown finished up the 1988 season by winning 10 of his final 12 decisions at Tulsa, with a sub-2.00 ERA.

He could be rushed into the big leagues right now, but with the winter addition of Nolan Ryan, the Rangers won't have to do that. Brown will probably go to Triple-A, where he can refine a changeup that he didn't throw in college because his fastball so overpowered hitters.

— **Tracy Ringolsby**

MINOR LEAGUE MENTIONS BY BA

YEAR	TOP 100	ORG RANKING	LEAGUE RANKING	BEST TOOLS
1987		**No. 1:** Rangers		
1988		**No. 4:** Rangers	**No. 6:** Texas	
1989		**No. 1:** Rangers		

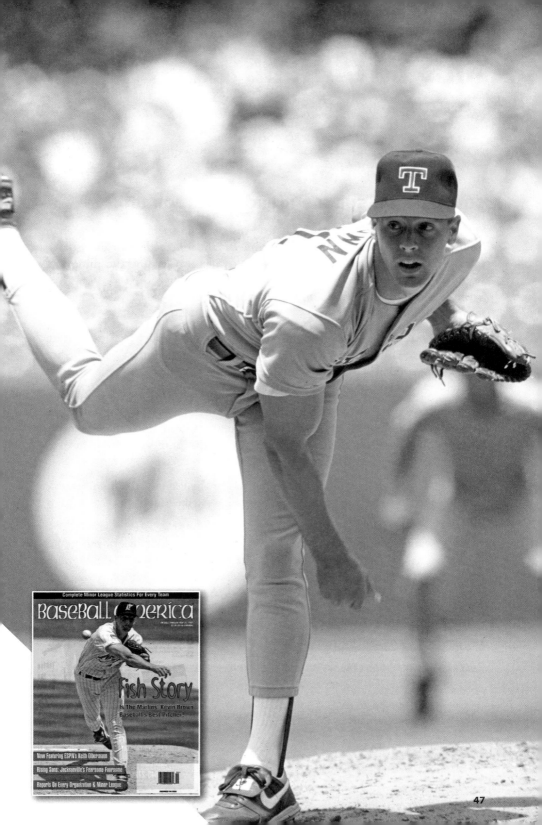

Complete Minor League Statistics For Every Team

BaseBall America

Fish Story

Is The Marlins' Kevin Brown
Baseball's Best Pitcher?

Now Featuring ESPN's Keith Olbermann

Rising Sons: Jacksonville's Foursome Foursome

Reports On Every Organization & Minor League

KRIS BRYANT, 3B

BIOGRAPHY

PROPER NAME: Kristopher Lee Bryant. **BORN:** January 4, 1992 in Las Vegas.
HT: 6-5. **WT:** 230. **BATS:** R. **THROWS:** R. **SCHOOL:** San Diego.
FIRST PRO CONTRACT: Selected by Cubs in first round (second overall)
of 2013 draft; signed July 12, 2013.

2014 MiLB PLAYER OF THE YEAR

SOUTHERN LEAGUE TOP 10 PROSPECTS FOR 2014

For the second straight year, a Cubs prospect who spent half the season at Tennessee led the minors in extra-base hits. Bryant collected 78 in all, surpassing by three Javier Baez's total from 2013, while also leading the minors in home runs (43), slugging (.661) and OPS (1.098). He earned a second-half promotion to Triple-A Iowa and won the BA Minor League Player of the Year award as well.

In the tradition of hard-hitting college third basemen such as Alex Gordon or Mark Teixeira, Bryant won't require much minor league time. While the hot corner might not be Bryant's ultimate position, Southern League evaluators favorably reviewed his double-plus arm and defensive agility.

Bryant's big righthanded bat will play no matter where he settles on the diamond. His leveraged, upper-cut swing is designed to launch the ball in the air with plus power to all fields, and half of his 22 homers in the Southern League went out either to center or right field.

One scout said Bryant had the fastest bat in the league, which will enable him to hit for average even though he projects to strike out as much as a quarter of the time.

"We wanted to pitch him away (to try to neutralize his power), but he hit the ball so hard the other way that we decided to go back inside," Chattanooga manager Razor Shines said. "That was a mistake, too. He's going to swing and miss, but if the pitcher doesn't hit his spots, then he's going to pay the price."

— **Matt Eddy**

MINOR LEAGUE MENTIONS BY BA

YEAR	TOP 100	ORG RANKING	LEAGUE RANKING	BEST TOOLS
2013			**No. 1:** Northwest	
2014	No. 8	**No. 2:** Cubs	**No. 1:** Southern **No. 1:** Pacific Coast	**SL:** Best Hitter, Best Power, Best INF Arm **PCL:** Best Defensive 3B
2015	No. 1	**No. 1:** Cubs		

MARK BUEHRLE, LHP

BIOGRAPHY

PROPER NAME: Mark Alan Buehrle. **BORN:** March 23, 1979 in St. Charles, Mo.
HT: 6-2. **WT:** 240. **BATS:** L. **THROWS:** L. **SCHOOL:** Jefferson (Mo.) JC.
FIRST PRO CONTRACT: Selected by White Sox in 38th round (1,139th overall) of 1998 draft;
signed May 21, 1999.

CHICAGO WHITE SOX TOP 10 PROSPECTS FOR 2000

BACKGROUND: As a 1998 draft-and-follow, Buehrle improved enough to not only sign for a low six-figure bonus but also get sent straight to Burlington, where he acquitted himself while pitching the Bees to a Midwest League title.

STRENGTHS: Buehrle has a complete assortment of pitches that he can throw for strikes, including an 88-90 mph fastball, two types of sliders, a curveball and changeup. The command of his breaking pitches is advanced for his age, and he consistently overmatched lefthanded hitters in the Midwest League.

WEAKNESSES: The White Sox are hard-pressed to identify a weakness in Buehrle. His fringe-average fastball may be his weakest pitch.

FUTURE: Buehrle could become the fastest-moving pitcher in the White Sox system. The organization has few lefthanded relievers, and though his five-pitch arsenal profiles him as a starter, short-term needs may put him in the bullpen almost immediately.

— **David Rawnsley**

SOUTHERN LEAGUE TOP 10 PROSPECTS FOR 2000

Buehrle has gone from anonymity to the majors in about a year. He gave up five earned runs in his first outing for Birmingham, then never gave up more than three in his next 15 starts, earning a promotion to Chicago.

"Buehrle is special because he's a four-pitch pitcher who can find the strike zone with all four pitches," Birmingham manager Nick Capra said.

He has no apparent weakness. Buehrle has an average fastball, terrific command of his curveball and slider, and a nifty changeup.

— **David Jenkins**

MINOR LEAGUE MENTIONS BY BA

YEAR	TOP 100	ORG RANKING	LEAGUE RANKING	BEST TOOLS
2000		**No. 10:** White Sox	**No. 9:** Southern	**SL:** Best Control

MADISON BUMGARNER, LHP

BIOGRAPHY

PROPER NAME: Madison Kyle Bumgarner. **BORN:** August 1, 1989 in Hickory, N.C.
HT: 6-4. **WT:** 242. **BATS:** R. **THROWS:** L. **SCHOOL:** South Caldwell HS, Hudson, N.C.
FIRST PRO CONTRACT: Selected by Giants in first round (10th overall) of 2007 draft;
signed Aug. 14, 2007.

SOUTH ATLANTIC LEAGUE TOP 10 PROSPECTS FOR 2008

The league's youngest starting pitcher as well as its pitcher of the year, Bumgarner was the first name mentioned by every manager who saw him, and for good reason.

After struggling with his revamped mechanics early in the season and surrendering 10 earned runs in his first 11.2 innings, the 10th overall pick from the 2007 draft returned to his high school delivery and didn't allow an earned run in his next four starts. Not only did he lead the minors in ERA, but he also won his both playoff starts while permitting just one unearned run in 14 innings.

"He's the most advanced pitcher I have ever seen at his age," Augusta manager Andy Skeels said. "His makeup is impressive, and he has every physical tool you could hope to have. He's the real deal, a true No. 1 starter at the major league level."

Bumgarner works with a fastball that sits at 94-95 mph and an ever-improving breaking ball and changeup. He pounds both sides of the plate and changes the batter's eye level with his ability to hit his spots with precision. He challenges hitters and exhibits a killer instinct on the mound.

"The way the ball comes out of his hand is incredible," Lexington manager Gregg Langbehn said. "We saw him early in the season and then late in the year. The second time, it wasn't much of a contest. He absolutely dominated us, especially with his ability to command his pitches on the inside part of the plate."

— **Jim Shonerd**

MINOR LEAGUE MENTIONS BY BA

YEAR	TOP 100	ORG RANKING	LEAGUE RANKING	BEST TOOLS
2008		**No. 3:** Giants	**No. 1:** South Atlantic	**SAL:** Best Pitching Prospect, Best Control
2009	No. 9	**No. 1:** Giants	**No. 2:** Eastern	**CAL:** Best Pitching Prospect
2010	No. 14	**No. 2:** Giants	**No. 4:** Pacific Coast	**PCL:** Best Pitching Prospect

MIGUEL CABRERA, 1B

BIOGRAPHY

PROPER NAME: Jose Miguel Cabrera. **BORN:** April 18, 1993 in Maracay, Venezuela.
HT: 6-4. **WT:** 249. **BATS:** R. **THROWS:** R. **SCHOOL:** Maracay, Venezuela.
FIRST PRO CONTRACT: Signed as international free agent by Marlins, July 2, 1999.

SOUTHERN LEAGUE TOP 10 PROSPECTS FOR 2003

As deep as the Southern League was, no league manager or scout considered anyone else for the top prospect spot. In fact, they had trouble restraining themselves from lavishing Cabrera with praise.

The lone complaint was the Cabrera knew he was too good for the league and it showed.

"His plate approach was outstanding for a 20-year-old," Tennessee manager Mark DeJohn said. "It's the approach to hitting you try to teach, but it comes natural to him. He uses the opposite field to drive in runs.

"It's the approach Albert Pujols uses. I'm not sure he has that kind of power, but he has that approach and he's very disciplined for a young hitter."

Cabrera pummeled lefthanders (.455 with five homers in 55 at-bats), which he continued to do in the big leagues.

Managers rated him the league's strongest infield arm and best defensive third baseman, though he made 15 errors in 64 games. He initially played left field in Florida after spending just three games there in Double-A, but moved back to third base after Mike Lowell's season-ending injury and made only one error in his first 20 starts there.

— **John Manuel**

MINOR LEAGUE MENTIONS BY BA

YEAR	TOP 100	ORG RANKING	LEAGUE RANKING	BEST TOOLS
2000		**No. 11:** Marlins		
2001	No. 91	**No. 3:** Marlins	**No. 9:** Midwest	**MWL:** Best INF Arm
2002	No. 38	**No. 2:** Marlins	**No. 5:** Florida State	
2003	No. 12	**No. 1:** Marlins	**No. 1:** Southern	**SL:** Best Hitter, Best Strike-Zone Judgment, Best Defensive 3B, Best INF Arm, Most Exciting Player

ROBINSON CANO, 2B

BIOGRAPHY

PROPER NAME: Robinson Jose Cano.
BORN: October 22, 1982 in San Pedro de Macoris, Dominican Republic.
HT: 6-0. **WT:** 210. **BATS:** L. **THROWS:** R. **SCHOOL:** San Pedro de Macoris, Dominican Republic.
FIRST PRO CONTRACT: Signed as international free agent by Yankees, Jan. 5, 2001.

NEW YORK YANKEES TOP 10 PROSPECTS FOR 2003

Cano's father, Jose, signed with the Yankees in 1980 and reached the big leagues with the Astros in 1989. The younger Cano played baseball and basketball at his Dominican high school, and from the first time he worked out for the Yankees has shown an advanced approach. Like Bronson Sardinha, he went to Staten Island after opening the 2002 season at low Class A Greensboro.

Cano's bat is his greatest strength. He generates plus bat speed and has a knack for making adjustments with his hands to put the barrel of the bat on balls in different zones. He covers the plate well with a good idea of the strike zone, makes consistent hard contact and projects to hit for power.

Defensively, Cano offers versatility, though he'll likely end up at second or third base or even right field with Ferdin Tejada and Joaquin Arias in the system. Cano has the actions, above-average arm and quick hands to play shortstop, and most of his errors were due to inexperience.

He's a below-average runner, but Cano finished third in the system in RBIs and should make the jump to high Class A in 2003.

— **Josh Boyd**

MINOR LEAGUE MENTIONS BY BA

YEAR	TOP 100	ORG RANKING	LEAGUE RANKING	BEST TOOLS
2002			**No. 11:** New York-Penn	
2003		**No. 8:** Yankees	**No. 18:** Florida State	**FSL:** Best Defensive 2B
2004		**No. 6:** Yankees	**No. 16:** Eastern **No. 14:** International	**EL:** Best Defensive 2B
2005		**No. 2:** Yankees		

CHRIS CARPENTER, RHP

BIOGRAPHY

PROPER NAME: Christopher John Carpenter. **BORN:** April 27, 1975 in Exeter, N.H.
HT: 6-6. **WT:** 230. **BATS:** R. **THROWS:** R. **SCHOOL:** Trinity HS, Manchester, N.H.
FIRST PRO CONTRACT: Selected by Blue Jays in first round (15th overall) of 1993 draft;
signed Aug. 10, 1993.

TORONTO BLUE JAYS TOP 10 PROSPECTS FOR 1997

BACKGROUND: Like so many Blue Jays prospects, Carpenter was a two-sport star in high school. He played hockey as well as baseball. He had back and arm problems in his first two pro seasons, but has proven durable the last two. He finished sixth in the Southern League in strikeouts in 1996.

STRENGTHS: Carpenter has athleticism and will do the little things to help himself. Most of all, he has stuff. He has developed a fastball that sits in the 92-93 mph range.

WEAKNESSES: Carpenter has a power curve that is a knee-buckler, but it has some extra play in it at times and needs to become more consistent. He still gets a little too excited, but has done a better job of harnessing his emotions. Getting to pitch regularly the last two years has been a big lift for him.

FUTURE: Carpenter is ready for the move to Triple-A in 1997, with a chance to force his way to the big leagues.

— **Tracy Ringolsby**

MINOR LEAGUE MENTIONS BY BA

YEAR	TOP 100	ORG RANKING	LEAGUE RANKING	BEST TOOLS
1994			**No. 3:** Pioneer	
1995	No. 100	**No. 5:** Blue Jays		
1996	No. 82	**No. 3:** Blue Jays		
1997	No. 28	**No. 3:** Blue Jays	**No. 10:** International	

ROGER CLEMENS, RHP

BIOGRAPHY

PROPER NAME: William Roger Clemens. **BORN:** August 4, 1962 in Dayton, Ohio.
HT: 6-4. **WT:** 235. **BATS:** R. **THROWS:** R. **SCHOOL:** Texas.
FIRST PRO CONTRACT: Selected by Red Sox in first round (19th overall) of 1983 draft; signed June 21, 1983.

EASTERN LEAGUE TOP 10 PROSPECTS FOR 1983

The 6-foot-3, 210 pound righthander from the University of Texas, Boston's No. 1 draft pick in June is considered a "can't-miss" kid. Clemens has four potential major league pitches: fastball, curveball, slider, and changeup.

"He has a great makeup for a pitcher," said one American League scout.

"He could be the best pitcher out of the draft. He'll be helping the Red Sox in a hurry—he's that good," said a National League scout.

New Britain manager Rac Slider called Clemens the best pitching prospect he's had in 23 years of managing in the minors.

— **Tom Shea**

BOSTON RED SOX TOP 10 PROSPECTS FOR 1984

The most accomplished pitcher from last June's draft, Clemens is expected to start the season in Triple-A, but some scouts say he is ready for the varsity rotation. If Dennis Eckersley is traded, part of the reason likely will be because the Red Sox think Clemens can fill the spot in the rotation.

In 11 pro starts last season after helping the Texas win the NCAA championship, Clemens had a 7-2 record, 1.33 ERA, 95 strikeouts and only 12 walks in 81 innings. He was equally dominant in both the Florida State League and the Eastern League.

Clemens' fastball approaches 90 mph, he has two speeds on his curveball, and he is developing a forkball that will serve as a changeup. Scouts say that his delivery is flawless—each pitch coming from the same motion—and that he puts the ball on a hitter's wrists as well as any young pitcher in years.

— **Ken Leiker**

MINOR LEAGUE MENTIONS BY BA

YEAR	TOP 100	ORG RANKING	LEAGUE RANKING	BEST TOOLS
1983			**No. 3:** Florida State **No. 1:** Eastern	**EL:** Best Control
1984		**No. 1:** Red Sox		

BETTMANN/GETTY IMAGES | ISSUE DATE: FEBRUARY, 1983

GERRIT COLE, RHP

BIOGRAPHY

PROPER NAME: Gerrit Alan Cole. **BORN:** September 8, 1990 in Newport Beach, Calif.
HT: 6-4. **WT:** 225. **BATS:** R. **THROWS:** R. **SCHOOL:** UCLA.
FIRST PRO CONTRACT: Selected by Pirates in first round (first overall) of 2011 draft;
signed Aug. 15, 2011.

ARIZONA FALL LEAGUE TOP 10 PROSPECTS FOR 2011

Cole was the first overall selection in the 2011 draft and, like [Mariners lefthander Danny] Hultzen, made his first pro appearance in Arizona. The UCLA product consistently hit triple digits with his heater and showed three plus pitches in his five AFL starts, generally looking like a pitcher worthy of being the No. 1 pick.

Like in college, he struggled at times with consistency of his command and feel for the breaking pitches; this tendency was especially evident in the Rising Stars game in which he gave up five runs and didn't make it out of the first inning. Cole's upside is higher, but scouts see Hultzen as more of a sure thing.

— **Bill Mitchell**

INTERNATIONAL LEAGUE TOP 10 PROSPECTS FOR 2013

The first overall pick in the draft by the Pirates two years ago, Cole is a promising front-line starter candidate with an unsurpassed arsenal. His primary weapons are a fastball that sits in the mid-90s and peaks at 100 mph, backed with a high-80s slider featuring tight rotation and sharp, darting movement.

"His fastball and breaking ball down in the zone is some of the best stuff I've seen this season," Indianapolis manager Dean Treanor said.

Cole's power stuff played just as well in the majors as it did at Triple-A. He keeps the ball in the park and showed the best control of his career in Pittsburgh. His changeup is firm, but usable.

One rival manager said Cole's stuff was similar in quality to the Mets' Matt Harvey, last year's standout starter prospect in the IL.

— **John Manuel**

MINOR LEAGUE MENTIONS BY BA

YEAR	TOP 100	ORG RANKING	LEAGUE RANKING	BEST TOOLS
2012	No. 12	**No. 1:** Pirates	**No. 2:** Florida State **No. 3:** Eastern	**FSL:** Best Fastball
2013	No. 7	**No. 1:** Pirates	**No. 3:** International	**IL:** Best Pitching Prospect

BARTOLO COLON, RHP

BIOGRAPHY

PROPER NAME: Bartolo Colon. **BORN:** May 24, 1973 in Altamira, Dominican Republic. **HT:** 5-11. **WT:** 285. **BATS:** R. **THROWS:** R. **SCHOOL:** Puerto Plata, Dominican Republic. **FIRST PRO CONTRACT:** Signed as international free agent by Indians, June 26, 1993.

CAROLINA LEAGUE TOP 10 PROSPECTS FOR 1995

Just two years removed from the Dominican Summer League, Colon was the hardest thrower in the league, and managers were impressed by his ability to maintain his plus fastball into the late innings.

Colon has exceptional control for a power pitcher. Not only does he not walk batters, but he can spot his fastball in the strike zone almost at will. He complements his heater with an improving curveball and a changeup.

The CL pitcher of the year kept getting better until a bone bruise in his pitching elbow shelved him for the last month of the season. At the time of his injury, he was leading the league in all three triple-crown categories.

"I haven't seen anyone with the stuff he's got," Kinston manager Gordy MacKenzie said. "He's got an exceptional arm. He just needs to pitch."

— **James Bailey**

EASTERN LEAGUE TOP 10 PROSPECTS FOR 1996

Colon, the top prospect in the Carolina League in 1995, spent much of '96 bothered by arm problems. When healthy, he showed a good fastball, such as in April, when 76 of his 92 pitches against Harrisburg were 90 mph or better.

"He's a kid who when he gets better command of his breaking ball is going to be a special kid with a power arm," Canton-Akron manager Jeff Datz said.

Cleveland promoted Colon to Triple-A late in the season and converted him to relief. The Indians believe a lesser workload may keep him healthier.

— **Andrew Linker**

MINOR LEAGUE MENTIONS BY BA

YEAR	TOP 100	ORG RANKING	LEAGUE RANKING	BEST TOOLS
1995			**No. 1:** Carolina	**CAR:** Best Pitching Prospect, Best Fastball
1996	No. 15	**No. 1:** Indians	**No. 8:** Eastern	**EL:** Best Pitching Prospect, Best Fastball
1997	No. 14	**No. 2:** Indians		

DAVID CONE, RHP

BIOGRAPHY

PROPER NAME: David Brian Cone. **BORN:** January 2, 1963 in Kansas City, Mo.
HT: 6-1. **WT:** 190. **BATS:** L. **THROWS:** R. **SCHOOL:** Rockhurst HS, Kansas City, Mo.
FIRST PRO CONTRACT: Selected by Royals in third round (74th overall) of 1981 draft;
signed June 10, 1981.

KANSAS CITY ROYALS TOP 10 PROSPECTS FOR 1985

Knee surgery forced Cone to miss 1983 and created concern about how well he could bounce back after a long layoff at such an early stage of his career.

The questions were answered in a hurry. Don't worry about the 8-12 record and 4.28 ERA or even the 114 walks. The stat to consider in evaluating Cone's return is that he led the Memphis team with 179 innings pitched and then had the second-lowest earned run average in the Florida Instructional League.

The knee never bothered him. He did appear to tire late in the season at Memphis but was strong again in the FIL. This will be a big season for Cone to show that, as well as being physically sound, he can regain command of his pitches. He has a plus fastball and adequate breaking pitches.

— **Tracy Ringolsby**

KANSAS CITY ROYALS TOP 10 PROSPECTS FOR 1986

After missing the 1983 season because of a major knee surgery, Cone has proven durable the last two years. He also showed that he still had the 90-plus mph fastball that led the Royals to make Cone a third-round selection in the 1981 draft, despite the fact his high school did not have a baseball team.

But he continued to struggle with control problems (207 walks in 338 innings), although it appears everything came together during the winter. Pitching in Puerto Rico, Cone had a 1-5 record, but his ERA was 2.26 and, more importantly, in 56 innings he cut his walks to 27 while striking out 45.

— **Tracy Ringolsby**

MINOR LEAGUE MENTIONS BY BA

YEAR	TOP 100	ORG RANKING	LEAGUE RANKING	BEST TOOLS
1983		**No. 6:** Royals		
1985		**No. 9:** Royals		
1986		**No. 3:** Royals		**AA:** Best Fastball, Best Reliever

Baseball america

BATTLE
OF THE
BIG APPLE

DAVID CONE
& BILL PULSIPHER
REPRESENT THE
YANKEES' & METS'
DIFFERENT
APPROACHES

JOHNNY CUETO, RHP

BIOGRAPHY

PROPER NAME: Johnny Cueto.
BORN: February 15, 1986 in San Pedro de Macoris, Dominican Republic.
HT: 5-11. **WT:** 229. **BATS:** R. **THROWS:** R.
FIRST PRO CONTRACT: Signed as international free agent by Reds, March 16, 2004.

CINCINNATI REDS TOP 10 PROSPECTS FOR 2008

Cueto was the first player signed out of the Dominican Republic after Cincinnati reworked its international scouting department in 2004. Thanks in part to working with former Reds star Mario Soto, Cueto hasn't taken long to become one of the system's gems.

Cueto pitches like a 10-year major league veteran, not a fresh-faced 21-year-old. He features a 93-94 mph fastball that touches 96 mph, a tight 83-88 mph slider and a solid changeup that he learned from Soto. His makeup is impeccable, which is why the Reds have felt comfortable keeping him on the fast track.

Cueto has above-average control, but he sometimes struggles with command in the strike zone. He found in his brief exposure to Triple-A that more advanced hitters will punish pitches up in the strike zone, even 94 mph fastballs.

The Reds plan on acquiring a veteran starter this offseason, which would leave Cueto without a clear spot in the rotation. He could bide his time waiting for an opening by helping out the Cincinnati bullpen.

— **J.J. Cooper**

MINOR LEAGUE MENTIONS BY BA

YEAR	TOP 100	ORG RANKING	LEAGUE RANKING	BEST TOOLS
2006			**No. 12:** Midwest **No. 14:** Florida State	
2007		**No. 4:** Reds	**No. 5:** Florida State **No. 4:** Southern	
2008	No. 34	**No. 4:** Reds		

JACOB DeGROM, RHP

BIOGRAPHY

PROPER NAME: Jacob Anthony deGrom. **BORN:** June 19, 1988 in De Leon Springs, Fla.
HT: 6-4. **WT:** 180. **BATS:** L. **THROWS:** R. **SCHOOL:** Stetson.
FIRST PRO CONTRACT: Selected by Mets in ninth round (272nd overall) of 2010 draft;
signed June 12, 2010.

NEW YORK METS TOP 10 PROSPECTS FOR 2013

DeGrom began his college career at Stetson as the starting shortstop, but he finished his time with the Hatters as the club's No. 1 starter. He first took the mound during his junior year, beginning as team's the closer but moving into the rotation down the stretch out of necessity. He had Tommy John surgery just a few months after signing for $95,000 as a ninth-rounder in 2010 and missed all of the following season.

DeGrom appeared no worse for the time off while making his full-season debut in 2012. His athleticism and clean arm action encourage scouts that he can refine his secondary pitches and stay in a starting role. His fastball is plenty good already. DeGrom carries 93-95 mph velocity through six innings, tops out at 98 mph and features solid sinking life.

He creates good angle and plane and has no trouble throwing strikes, as evidenced by his rate of 1.6 walks per nine innings last year. His slider could develop into a plus weapon if he succeeds in getting more lateral break on the pitch. That's a possibility because he generates plenty of tight spin now. He'll need to continue honing his feel for a changeup.

Though he's much less experienced than the typical 24-year-old pitching prospect, deGrom's feel for a sinker and slider make him a potential No. 3 or 4 starter. He may begin 2013 in high Class A, but look for him to receive ample Double-A experience during the year.

— **Matt Eddy**

MINOR LEAGUE MENTIONS BY BA

YEAR	TOP 100	ORG RANKING	LEAGUE RANKING	BEST TOOLS
2013		**No. 11:** Mets		
2014		**No. 10:** Mets		

CARLOS DELGADO, 1B

BIOGRAPHY

PROPER NAME: Carlos Juan Delgado. **BORN:** June 25, 1972 in Aguadilla, Puerto Rico.
HT: 6-3. **WT:** 245. **BATS:** L. **THROWS:** R. **SCHOOL:** Aguadilla, Puerto Rico.
FIRST PRO CONTRACT: Signed as international free agent by Blue Jays, Oct. 9, 1988.

NEW YORK-PENN LEAGUE TOP 10 PROSPECTS FOR 1990

Delgado has everything scouts look for in a young catcher: a strong arm, aggressiveness behind the plate, intelligence and a decent bat.

"He's a franchise catcher," said one member of the Blue Jays' player development program. "He's not just a prospect, he's the No. 1 prospect in our whole organization."

— **Peter Conradi**

TORONTO BLUE JAYS TOP 10 PROSPECTS FOR 1992

Delgado's bat will be his ticket to the big leagues. He has plus power. After two years at the short-season level, he made his presence felt at Myrtle Beach with 18 home runs among his 38 extra-base hits. For a younger player, he also shows decent plate discipline, drawing 75 walks to offset 97 strikeouts.

The question of position is one the Jays can answer as Delgado moves up in the system. For now, he will be given every chance to catch.

He has a strong arm. What isn't as certain is whether he will develop into a solid receiver. With his size, he'll have to work constantly to keep his mechanics in sync.

— **Tracy Ringolsby**

MINOR LEAGUE MENTIONS BY BA

YEAR	TOP 100	ORG RANKING	LEAGUE RANKING	BEST TOOLS
1990			**No. 4:** New York-Penn	
1991		**No. 6:** Blue Jays	**No. 3:** South Atlantic	
1992	No. 67	**No. 5:** Blue Jays	**No. 1:** Florida State	**FSL:** Best Hitter, Best Power
1993	No. 4	**No. 1:** Blue Jays	**No. 2:** Southern	**SL:** Best Hitter, Best Power
1994	No. 5	**No. 2:** Blue Jays	**No. 3:** International	
1995			**No. 7:** International	

Baseball
America

ON SALE THROUGH MAY 15, 1994

FRESH
FACES

LOOK WHO'S
IN LEFT FIELD
FOR TORONTO:
CARLOS
DELGADO

HECTOR
CARRASCO,
TIM DAVIS
JUMP TO
THE BIGS
FROM
CLASS A

CLIFF FLOYD:
THE MAN BEHIND
THE HYPE

TOP 25
HIGH SCHOOL
PROSPECTS

LAST
LAUGH

BLUE JAYS
GENERAL MANAGER
PAT GILLICK
RETIRES ON TOP

73

FREDDIE FREEMAN, 1B

BIOGRAPHY

PROPER NAME: Frederick Charles Freeman. **BORN:** September 12, 1989 in Fountain Valley, Calif.
HT: 6-5. **WT:** 220. **BATS:** L. **THROWS:** R. **SCHOOL:** El Modena HS, Orange, Calif.
FIRST PRO CONTRACT: Selected by Braves in second round (78th overall) of 2007 draft;
signed June 10, 2007.

ATLANTA BRAVES TOP 10 PROSPECTS FOR 2009

Many scouts preferred Freeman as a power pitching prospect, but he wanted to swing the bat and the Braves were glad to oblige when they drafted him in the second round in 2007. The youngest player to sign out of the 2007 draft, he was named the Braves' minor league player of the year in 2008 after ranking second in the South Atlantic League in slugging (.521) and fourth in RBIs (95).

Freeman is an RBI machine who relishes the opportunity to hit with runners on base. He's an aggressive hitter with a swing-first approach, yet he has good pitch recognition and doesn't chase pitches out of the zone. He drives the ball with authority with his sweet, smooth swing and should be able to produce significant home run totals at higher levels.

His defense is well above-average at first base, with some scouts comparing Freeman to Mark Grace but with more power. Freeman's approach doesn't lend itself to drawing a lot of walks. He has below-average speed, though he's by no means a baseclogger.

The Braves could have moved Freeman to high Class A last season with relative ease, but they wanted to make certain he had a solid foundation of success as an 18-year-old. He'll move up to Myrtle Beach in 2009, and the Braves won't hold him back if he continues to produce.

— **Bill Ballew**

MINOR LEAGUE MENTIONS BY BA

YEAR	TOP 100	ORG RANKING	LEAGUE RANKING	BEST TOOLS
2008		**No. 19:** Braves	**No. 10:** South Atlantic	
2009	No. 87	**No. 5:** Braves	**No. 4:** Carolina **No. 8:** Southern	**CAR:** Best Defensive 1B **SL:** Best Defensive 1B
2010	No. 32	**No. 2:** Braves	**No. 5:** International	**IL:** Best Defensive 1B
2011	No. 17	**No. 2:** Braves		

ERIC GAGNE, RHP

BIOGRAPHY

PROPER NAME: Eric Serge Gagne. **BORN:** January 7, 1976 in Montreal, Canada.
HT: 6-0. **WT:** 240. **BATS:** R. **THROWS:** R. **SCHOOL:** Seminole State (Okla.) JC.
FIRST PRO CONTRACT: Signed as nondrafted free agent by Dodgers, July 26, 1995.

LOS ANGELES DODGERS TOP 10 PROSPECTS FOR 2000

BACKGROUND: Gagne, a member of the Canadian national junior team, was passed over in the 1995 draft and signed that summer. He missed the 1997 season after Tommy John surgery. He rebounded to lead all of Double-A in strikeouts and fewest hits per nine innings in 1999.

STRENGTHS: Gagne has a long, fluid, three-quarter arm action, lending heavy sink to his 90-92 mph fastball. His changeup, an outstanding pitch he uses to close out hitters, gets similar sinking action from the same release point. The Dodgers describe Gagne's demeanor as tough, though opponents lean toward mean.

WEAKNESSES: Gagne's curveball lags behind his fastball and changeup. He had eye surgery following the season to correct problems that forced him to wear heavy goggles on the mound.

FUTURE: The previous regime didn't consider Gagne a prospect, but his performance in 1999 changed that. He is likely to start 2000 in the Dodgers' rotation.

— **David Rawnsley**

MINOR LEAGUE MENTIONS BY BA

YEAR	TOP 100	ORG RANKING	LEAGUE RANKING	BEST TOOLS
1999			**No. 6:** Texas	
2000	No. 49	**No. 2:** Dodgers		

NOMAR GARCIAPARRA, SS

BIOGRAPHY

PROPER NAME: Anthony Nomar Garciaparra. **BORN:** July 23, 1973 in Whittier, Calif.
HT: 6-0. **WT:** 165. **BATS:** R. **THROWS:** R. **SCHOOL:** Georgia Tech.
FIRST PRO CONTRACT: Selected by Red Sox in first round (12th overall) of 1994 draft;
signed July 20, 1994.

BOSTON RED SOX TOP 10 PROSPECTS FOR 1996

BACKGROUND: The only freshman ever to start for the U.S. Olympic team (1992), Garciaparra signed with the Red Sox for $895,000. He was named the Eastern League's best defensive shortstop and best baserunner in 1995.

STRENGTHS: Garciaparra is known for his defense. He has excellent range, especially to his left, an above-average arm and a quick release. His intelligence makes him a better hitter and runner than his tools would indicate. He projects as No. 2 hitter with 20-25 steals per year.

WEAKNESSES: The slightly built Garciaparra wore down in 1995, necessitating conditioning work this offseason. To be a No. 2 hitter, he'll have to be more selective and draw more walks.

FUTURE: If the Red Sox didn't have Jose Valentin, Garciaparra would be their Opening Day starter. Instead, he'll play at Triple-A Pawtucket before pushing Valentin to third base in 1997.

— **Jim Callis**

INTERNATIONAL LEAGUE TOP 10 PROSPECTS FOR 1996

Before he was promoted to Boston late in the year, Garciaparra's playing time was limited by knee injuries. When he was healthy, he excelled.

"He's a possible franchise player," Toledo manager Tom Runnells said.

One manager didn't care for Garciaparra's throwing mechanics. But that was the only dislike on a long list of likes: great hands, good arm, good range, good contact, increased strength and developing power.

— **Tim Pearrell**

MINOR LEAGUE MENTIONS BY BA

YEAR	TOP 100	ORG RANKING	LEAGUE RANKING	BEST TOOLS
1995	No. 22	**No. 1:** Red Sox	**No. 4:** Eastern	**EL:** Best Baserunner, Best Defensive SS
1996	No. 36	**No. 4:** Red Sox	**No. 1:** International	
1997	No. 10	**No. 1:** Red Sox		

JASON GIAMBI, 1B

BIOGRAPHY

PROPER NAME: Jason Gilbert Giambi. **BORN:** January 8, 1971 in West Covina, Calif.
HT: 6-3. **WT:** 240. **BATS:** L. **THROWS:** R. **SCHOOL:** Long Beach State.
FIRST PRO CONTRACT: Selected by the Athletics in second round (58th overall) of 1992 draft;
signed July 3, 1992.

CALIFORNIA LEAGUE TOP 10 PROSPECTS FOR 1993

Like Calvin Murray, a 1992 U.S. Olympian, Giambi started strong but was sidelined by a thumb injury for most of the second half. He has good hitting ability, excellent plate discipline (73 walks, 47 strikeouts) and was named the league's best defensive third baseman.

"He's a good contact hitter with occasional power," [Stockton Ports manager Lamar] Johnson said. "He did a good job against us at third."

— **Maureen Delany**

OAKLAND ATHLETICS TOP 10 PROSPECTS FOR 1995

BACKGROUND: The 1992 Olympian has shown just about everything to make an offensive player offensive, most notably a .318 average after moving to Triple-A in 1994.

STRENGTHS: Despite only 10 home runs in '94 and 16 the previous season, Giambi is considered a legitimate power source. Thumb and hand injuries have cut into his power. He also is probably the A's best potential average hitter. He could hit .300 in the big leagues with a high on-base percentage.

WEAKNESSES: All that separates Giambi from the majors is defense. He has shown improvement as he has moved through the system, but he made 19 errors in 89 games at third base in 1994.

FUTURE: Giambi is almost ready offensively. If his glove work has improved, he could win the third-base job in spring training. More likely, he will spend the year at Triple-A Edmonton.

— **Casey Tefertiller**

MINOR LEAGUE MENTIONS BY BA

YEAR	TOP 100	ORG RANKING	LEAGUE RANKING	BEST TOOLS
1993			**No. 9:** California	**CAL:** Best Defensive 3B
1995		**No. 4:** Athletics		

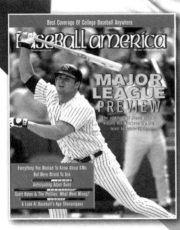

TOM GLAVINE, LHP

BIOGRAPHY

PROPER NAME: Thomas Michael Glavine. **BORN:** March 25, 1966 in Concord, Mass.
HT: 6-0. **WT:** 205. **BATS:** L. **THROWS:** L. **SCHOOL:** Billerica (Mass.) HS.
FIRST PRO CONTRACT: Selected by Braves in second round (47th overall) of 1984 draft;
signed June 22, 1984.

SOUTHERN LEAGUE TOP 10 PROSPECTS FOR 1986

He's a mere pup by age (19) standards, but Glavine—twice the greater Boston scholar-athlete of the year—is developed beyond his years on the mound.

Drafted out of Billerica (Mass.) High School by both the Braves and the NHL's Los Angeles Kings, Glavine continued his steady progress in the Braves' system this year, posting a 3.41 ERA before earning a promotion to Triple-A.

"Outstanding poise for his age and experience, in a tough league," is what Columbus manager Gary Tuck said of Glavine.

— **Larry Fleming**

ATLANTA BRAVES TOP 10 PROSPECTS FOR 1987

Growing up in the Boston area, Glavine's baseball experience was limited. He spent more time on the ice than the baseball field — and was a fourth-round choice of the NHL's Los Angeles Kings in addition to being the Braves' second-round selection in the 1984 draft.

Glavine has, however, developed quickly since devoting his attention to baseball, spending the bulk of last year at Double-A Greenville, where his 3.41 ERA ranked fourth in the Southern League.

Despite being young, a lefthander and not from an area with an emphasis on baseball, Glavine has command of all four pitches, including a sinking fastball that runs. His biggest asset, however, is his knowledge of pitching. He's the type of pitcher who can win games on days when he doesn't have good stuff because he will think his way through a game and remain in command of his emotions—regardless of the situation.

— **Tracy Ringolsby**

MINOR LEAGUE MENTIONS BY BA

YEAR	TOP 100	ORG RANKING	LEAGUE RANKING	BEST TOOLS
1985		**No. 3:** Braves	**No. 6:** South Atlantic	
1986		**No. 2:** Braves	**No. 2:** Southern	
1987		**No. 2:** Braves		

PAUL GOLDSCHMIDT, 1B

BIOGRAPHY

PROPER NAME: Paul Edward Goldschmidt. **BORN:** September 10, 1987 in Wilmington, Del.
HT: 6-3. **WT:** 225. **BATS:** R. **THROWS:** R. **SCHOOL:** Texas State.
FIRST PRO CONTRACT: Selected by D-backs in 8th round (246th overall) of 2009 draft;
signed June 14, 2009.

CALIFORNIA LEAGUE TOP 20 PROSPECTS FOR 2010

Goldschmidt's power became the stuff of legend around the Cal League, as nearly everyone he faced witnessed him hitting balls a long way. The league MVP, he led the the the circuit in doubles (42), homers (35), extra-base hits (80), total bases (318) and slugging (.606).

More than just a pull hitter, Goldschmidt has power to all fields. He ranked second in the league with 161 strikeouts, and while some observers thought the whiffs were an acceptable tradeoff for his homers, others think he'll make less contact at higher levels because he struggles with high fastballs and pulls off breaking pitches. He's a well below-average runner and athlete who's limited to first base, where he's an adequate defender.

— **Josh Leventhal**

SOUTHERN LEAGUE TOP 10 PROSPECTS FOR 2011

The MVP of the high Class A California League last year, Goldschmidt added a Southern League MVP trophy to his collection this year.

Goldschmidt has outstanding balance and doesn't have many moving parts in his swing, so there's minimal wasted effort getting his swing started. He's strong, keeps his weight back and stays within his swing, driving the ball for plus-plus power to all fields. He's prone to chasing high fastballs and will always have a high strikeout rate, but he'll also draw plenty of walks.

Though he's a well below-average runner, Goldschmidt has worked to improve his defense and become close to an average first baseman. He has gotten better at picking balls in the dirt and turning the double play.

— **Ben Badler**

MINOR LEAGUE MENTIONS BY BA

YEAR	TOP 100	ORG RANKING	LEAGUE RANKING	BEST TOOLS
2010		**No. 13:** D-backs	**No. 17:** California	**CAL:** Best Power
2011		**No. 11:** D-backs	**No. 3:** Southern	**SL:** Best Hitter, Best Power, Best Strike-Zone Judgment, Best Defensive 1B, Most Exciting Player

JUAN GONZALEZ, OF

BIOGRAPHY

PROPER NAME: Juan Alberto Gonzalez. **BORN:** October 20, 1969 in Arecibo, Puerto Rico.
HT: 6-3. **WT:** 220. **BATS:** R. **THROWS:** R. **SCHOOL:** Vega Baja, Puerto Rico.
FIRST PRO CONTRACT: Signed as international free agent by Rangers, May 30, 1986.

SOUTH ATLANTIC LEAGUE TOP 10 PROSPECTS FOR 1987

Gonzalez, it seems to be agreed upon, has the talent. The question is his temper and maturity.

Said [Macon manager Dennis] Rogers of Gonzalez, a high-priced Puerto Rican signee: "I've heard this [criticism] about his maturity and work habits. I had Jose Canseco in the minor leagues, and they were saying the same things about him. Let's give him time."

— **Richard Chesley**

TEXAS RANGERS TOP 10 PROSPECTS FOR 1990

Gonzalez has been considered a future star from the day he signed. He always has been the youngest player in his league, and in his first three years had to battle to stay competitive.

Not in 1989. He took the Texas League by storm, hitting .293 with 21 homers and 30 doubles, both of which were third-best in the league. Most importantly, Gonzalez made adjustments and got better as the season progressed.

Still a rather gangly kid, Gonzalez took a major step this winter with regular playing time in the Puerto Rican League.

Gonzalez is far from the prototype center fielder, but he has good enough and slightly above-average speed. As he fills out, Gonzalez might lose a step and may wind up in left or right. But that won't be a problem. He has the arm to play right and shows the offensive potential to be dominating in any spot.

— **Tracy Ringolsby**

MINER LEAGUE MENTIONS BY BA				
YEAR	**TOP 100**	**ORG RANKING**	**LEAGUE RANKING**	**BEST TOOLS**
1987		**No. 6:** Rangers	**No. 10:** South Atlantic	**SAL:** Best Defensive OF
1988		**No. 1:** Rangers		
1989		**No. 3:** Rangers	**No. 4:** Texas	**TL:** Best OF Arm
1990		**No. 1:** Rangers	**No. 1:** American Association	**AA:** Best Hitter, Best Power, Best OF Arm

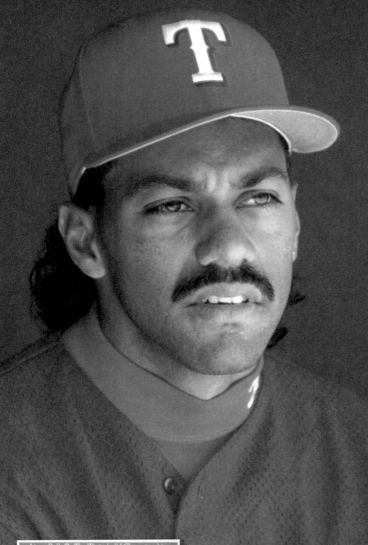

DWIGHT GOODEN, RHP

1983 MiLB PLAYER OF THE YEAR

NEW YORK METS TOP 10 PROSPECTS FOR 1983

The 6-foot-5, 200 pound righthander was the Mets' top draft pick last June. At age 17, Gooden was 5-4 with a 2.47 ERA for Kingsport (Appalachian) and averaged better than a strikeout per inning in his first season of pro ball.

He has an outstanding arm, excellent arm action and tops 90 miles per hour with his fastball. He also has tremendous poise for his age. Gooden only needs to gain experience as he advances through the organization.

— Ron Morris

CAROLINA LEAGUE TOP 10 PROSPECTS FOR 1983

His 300 strikeouts and 19-4 record speak for themselves.

At age 18 (19 in November), scouts and managers believe Gooden could be ready for the major leagues as early as next season. The Mets have said they will give every chance to make the big club in spring training.

Gooden has an outstanding curveball to go with 90-95 mph fastball. He just needs to work on his pickoff moves and holding runners on base.

— Ron Morris

MINOR LEAGUE MENTIONS BY BA

YEAR	TOP 100	ORG RANKING	LEAGUE RANKING	BEST TOOLS
1982			**No. 2:** Appalachian	
1983		**No. 4:** Mets	**No. 1:** Carolina	**CAR:** Best Fastball, Best Pitching Prospect
1984		**No. 1:** Mets		

ZACK GREINKE, RHP

BIOGRAPHY

PROPER NAME: Donald Zackary Greinke. **BORN:** October 21, 1983 in Orlando.
HT: 6-2. **WT:** 200. **BATS:** R. **THROWS:** R. **SCHOOL:** Apopka (Fla.) HS.
FIRST PRO CONTRACT: Selected by Royals in first round (sixth overall) of 2002 draft;
signed July 13, 2002.

CAROLINA LEAGUE TOP 10 PROSPECTS FOR 2003

Believe the hype. Everywhere Greinke went in the league, he drew rave reviews for his Greg Maddux-like command and his bulldog mentality on the mound. Greinke befuddled hitters by altering speeds on his fastball and curveball. He also throws a slider and changeup and can throw any of the pitches for strikes in any count.

"He's overpowering physically and mentally," Kinston manager Torey Lovullo said. "He did a great job of attacking hitters and changing speeds. He'd throw his fastball one time and hit 95, then drop it back to 80. He's as close to what you'd call a sure thing as I've seen."

—Chris Kline

TEXAS LEAGUE TOP 10 PROSPECTS FOR 2003

Greinke established himself as one of the best pitching prospects in the minors this year. He wasn't quite as dominant in the TL as he was in the Carolina League, but managers were still impressed with all he can do as a 19-year-old.

Beyond any of his stuff, Greinke earned kudos for his command, poise and feel for pitching. He's mature beyond his years, he can throw any of his pitches just about anywhere he wants, and he changes speeds masterfully. His stuff isn't short by any means—his fastball touches 93 mph and he's young enough that he could add velocity.

"A 19-year-old shouldn't have that kind of command," [San Antonio manager Dave] Brundage said. "A 19-year-old shouldn't be able to throw wherever you want, whenever you want."

— Will Lingo

MINOR LEAGUE MENTIONS BY BA				
YEAR	TOP 100	ORG RANKING	LEAGUE RANKING	BEST TOOLS
2003	No. 54	**No. 1:** Royals	**No. 1:** Carolina **No. 2:** Texas	**CAR:** Best Pitching Prospect, Best Control
2004	No. 14	**No. 1:** Royals		

KEN GRIFFEY JR., OF

BIOGRAPHY

PROPER NAME: George Kenneth Griffey Jr. **BORN:** November 21, 1969 in Donora, Pa.
HT: 6-2. **WT:** 230. **BATS:** L. **THROWS:** L. **SCHOOL:** Archbishop Moeller HS, Cincinnati.
FIRST PRO CONTRACT: Selected by Mariners in first round (first overall) of 1987 draft;
signed June 2, 1987.

NORTHWEST LEAGUE TOP 10 PROSPECTS FOR 1987

Who is the best major league prospect in the Northwest League?

Boy, what a stupid question. If Ken Griffey Jr. isn't the best prospect in the NWL, then Tommy Lasorda doesn't have a fondness for lasagna.

The amazing thing about the 6-foot-3, 190-pound Griffey is his ability to handle pitchers three of four years his elder. Don't forget, he is only 17 years old and was sent straight to the Bellingham Mariners after Seattle picked him first overall in the June draft from Cincinnati's Moeller High School.

Griffey suffered homesickness and missed part of the season with injuries, but he left a lasting impression on those who saw him play.

The only manager who didn't vote Griffey No. 1 agreed he was the best prospect but left him off his list because of "questionable work habits."

Griffey can run, throw, play the outfield, hit for average and hit for power.

Need to know more?

"He has better tools right now than most major leaguers," Bellingham manager Rick Sweet said. "Experience is the only thing that he lacks."

To watch Griffey hit a homer is to watch a ball jump off the bat and tower over the right-field fence.

"He can do anything he wants," Spokane manager Rob Picciolo said.

"He has all the tools to be a superstar," added Everett's Joe Strain.

— **Vince Bruun**

MINOR LEAGUE MENTIONS BY BA

YEAR	TOP 100	ORG RANKING	LEAGUE RANKING	BEST TOOLS
1987			No. 1: Northwest	
1988		No. 1: Mariners	No. 1: California	CAL: Best Hitter, Best Power, Best Defensive OF
1989		No. 1: Mariners		

Predicting The Races: Mets, Padres, Jays, A's

Major League Organization Reports

Baseball America

"Baseball News You Can't Get Anywhere Else"

April 28-May 9, 1989

Price $1.89 ($2.50 In Canada)

Now In Our 9th Year

Ken Griffey Jr. Sprints Into The Big Time

Top Pro Prospects By Position

Draft '89: Top College Prospects

Camp Reports: Florida, Arizona

Complete College Coverage

VLADIMIR GUERRERO, OF

BIOGRAPHY

PROPER NAME: Vladimir Guerrero. **BORN:** February 9, 1975 in Nizao, Dominican Republic.
HT: 6-3. **WT:** 235. **BATS:** R. **THROWS:** R. **SCHOOL:** Nizao, Dominican Republic.
FIRST PRO CONTRACT: Signed as international free agent by Montreal Expos, March 1, 1993.

GULF COAST LEAGUE TOP 10 PROSPECTS FOR 1994

Guerrero arrived late because he was busy hammering 12 home runs in the Dominican Summer League. One traveled more than 450 feet.

"He reminds you of a young Andre Dawson," Marlins manager Juan Bustabad said. "He has outstanding bat speed."

Guerrero is a free swinger, but there's hope he'll learn discipline at the plate. He tracks fly balls well in center and has above-average arm strength.

— **Allan Simpson**

MONTREAL EXPOS TOP 10 PROSPECTS FOR 1995

BACKGROUND: Signed with little fanfare, Guerrero turned the Rookie-level Dominican Summer League on its ear in 1994. He continued to excel when he was brought stateside to finish the season.

STRENGTHS: Guerrero may have the greatest upside potential of any Expos prospect, and it would surprise no one if he moved to No. 1 on this list a year from now. His power and arm strength rate a 7 on the scouting 2-8 scale, and he has no glaring weakness at the plate.

WEAKNESSES: Guerrero runs well but has long, loping strides and doesn't know how to use his speed yet on either offense or defense.

FUTURE: The Expos prefer to start their best outfield prospects in center field and let them play themselves out of the position. They think it will be at least two years before Guerrero switches to right.

— **Allan Simpson**

MINOR LEAGUE MENTIONS BY BA

YEAR	TOP 100	ORG RANKING	LEAGUE RANKING	BEST TOOLS
1994			No. 4: Gulf Coast	
1995	No. 85	No. 5: Expos	No. 2: South Atlantic	SAL: Best OF Arm
1996	No. 9	No. 1: Expos	No. 1: Eastern	EL: Best Hitter, Best Power, Best Defensive OF, Best OF Arm, Most Exciting Player
1997	No. 2	No. 1: Expos		

BaseBall america

PETER GAMMONS
ON THE CLASSIC
1988 POSTSEASON

PROSPECTS

The Best In Every Minor League

EXPOS
PHENOM
VLADIMIR
GUERRERO:
NO. 1 IN THE EASTERN LEAGUE

ROY HALLADAY, RHP

BIOGRAPHY

PROPER NAME: Harry Leroy Halladay. **BORN:** May 14, 1977 in Denver.
HT: 6-6. **WT:** 225. **BATS:** R. **THROWS:** R. **SCHOOL:** Arvada (Colo.) West HS.
FIRST PRO CONTRACT: Selected by Blue Jays in first round (17th overall) of 1995 draft;
signed June 30, 1995.

TORONTO BLUE JAYS TOP 10 PROSPECTS FOR 1996

BACKGROUND: Halladay is the latest in a line of top high school pitchers from Colorado. The state also produced first-round picks Scott Elarton and Jayson Peterson in 1994. Halladay finished third in the state high school cross-country championships.

STRENGTHS: Halladay has the legitimate fastball, but his big pitch is a knuckle-curve that has the potential to be his out-pitch in the big leagues.

WEAKNESSES: From Colorado, Halladay's exposure is limited because of the long winters. He's at his best when he keeps his 93 mph fastball down in the zone. He needs to throw his knuckle-curve more consistently for strikes.

FUTURE: Halladay figures to step into the South Atlantic League for a year of work at the full-season Class A level. He could move to the Florida State League at midyear.

— **Tracy Ringolsby**

INTERNATIONAL LEAGUE TOP 10 PROSPECTS FOR 1998

Halladay was No. 5 on this list last year, but he looked even better on his way to the Blue Jays' rotation. "He's nasty," Buffalo first baseman Jeff Manto said. "He's got the nastiest stuff in the league."

This season, Halladay learned to pitch inside, threw a sharper slider and worked on improving his changeup. He already had a good fastball, but now he's getting more down movement and recording more groundball outs.

— **Lacy Lusk and Matt Michael**

MINOR LEAGUE MENTIONS BY BA

YEAR	TOP 100	ORG RANKING	LEAGUE RANKING	BEST TOOLS
1995			**No. 5:** Gulf Coast	
1996		**No. 6:** Blue Jays	**No. 3:** Florida State	
1997	No. 23	**No. 1:** Blue Jays	**No. 5:** International	**IL:** Best Fastball
1998	No. 38	**No. 1:** Blue Jays	**No. 3:** International	**IL:** Best Fastball
1999	No. 12	**No. 1:** Blue Jays		

COLE HAMELS, LHP

BIOGRAPHY

PROPER NAME: Colbert Michael Hamels. **BORN:** December 27, 1983 in San Diego.
HT: 6-4. **WT:** 205. **BATS:** L. **THROWS:** L. **SCHOOL:** Rancho Bernardo HS, San Diego.
FIRST PRO CONTRACT: Selected by Phillies in first round (17th overall) of 2002 draft;
signed Aug. 28, 2002.

PHILADELPHIA PHILLIES TOP 10 PROSPECTS FOR 2003

Some clubs considered Hamels the best pitcher in the 2002 draft, but his medical history allowed the Phillies to get him with the 17th overall pick.

Hamels' fastball reaches 94 mph with good life, though he often pitches closer to 90. He shows exceptional control of his curveball and already has a solid changeup. Hamels has an easy delivery and advanced feel for pitching.

Hamels might have a better feel for pitching than Gavin Floyd and Brett Myers did at the same stage of their careers. He could make his pro debut in low Class A and move quickly from there.

— **Will Kimmey**

SOUTH ATLANTIC LEAGUE TOP 10 PROSPECTS FOR 2003

Another 2002 first-rounder who signed late, Hamels started the season in extended spring training. After putting several dominant starts together there, Hamels went to Lakewood in May.

Hamels pitches with average velocity but can dial it up to 92-94 mph with two strikes. He relies on a plus-plus changeup to keep hitters off-balance. His curveball needs refinement, as he doesn't always get consistent hard snap on it.

"The best arm I've seen in the league by far," a National League scout said. "The secondary stuff is what set him apart from the other guys. He has great life on his stuff. He was a man among boys. Nobody had this type of command and quality of three secondary pitches."

— **Josh Boyd**

MINOR LEAGUE MENTIONS BY BA

YEAR	TOP 100	ORG RANKING	LEAGUE RANKING	BEST TOOLS
2003		**No. 5:** Phillies	**No. 3:** South Atlantic	**SAL:** Best Breaking Pitch
2004	No. 17	**No. 1:** Phillies		
2005	No. 71	**No. 3:** Phillies		
2006	No. 68	**No. 1:** Phillies		

BRYCE HARPER, OF

BIOGRAPHY

PROPER NAME: Bryce Aron Max Harper. **BORN:** October 16, 1992 in Las Vegas.
HT: 6-3. **WT:** 220. **BATS:** L. **THROWS:** R. **SCHOOL:** JC of Southern Nevada.
FIRST PRO CONTRACT: Selected by Nationals in first round (first overall) of 2010 draft;
signed August 16, 2010.

EASTERN LEAGUE TOP 10 PROSPECTS FOR 2011

The league's youngest player by 15 months, Harper overcame the first extended slump of his pro career, a 1-for-25 slide, to finish with more than respectable numbers. A hamstring injury ended his season two weeks early, but he made a strong impression in his short time.

Harper has excellent strength and bat speed and near-legendary power. He refined his two-strike mindset and learned to spread out and let balls travel deeper, an approach that culminated with a game-winning, 450-foot homer over the batter's eye in center field against Trenton on Aug. 12. He does have some excessive movement in his swing that gives scouts and managers pause while grading his hit tool, though his fearsome presence ensures that he'll draw plenty of walks.

A former catcher who played center and right field in low Class A, Harper moved to left field for the first time when he got to Harrisburg. He made quick adjustments after some early struggles, using his plus-plus arm to pick up seven assists in 37 games. He also has slighty above-average speed and an intense nature on the bases and on defense.

"He's a throwback with off-the-charts ability," Erie manager Cris Cron said. "He has it all and has it at such an early age. He flat-out attacks the ball with a very solid approach. He's figured it out so early in his life, when it takes some a lifetime. I love the aggressiveness to his game"

— **John Manuel**

MINOR LEAGUE MENTIONS BY BA

YEAR	TOP 100	ORG RANKING	LEAGUE RANKING	BEST TOOLS
2011	No. 1	**No. 1:** Nationals	**No. 1:** South Atlantic **No. 1:** Eastern	**SAL:** Best Hitter, Best Power, Most Exciting Player
2012	No. 1	**No. 1:** Nationals		

BaseBall america

MAJORS · MINORS · PROSPECTS · DRAFT · COLLEGE · HIGH SCHOOL

DRAFT PREVIEW

PLUS

More Than 100
Scouting Reports,
Plus Top Prospects
At Each Position

Lining Up The First
Round Beyond
Harper To Nationals

James Paxton
Follows Well-Worn
Path To Indy Ball

Zack Cox Emerges
As Top College
Hitter, While
Jameson Taillon
Leads High School
Arms

Baseball Mourns
Ernie Harwell,
Robin Roberts

BEYOND
the HYPE

SEPARATE FACT FROM FICTION
WITH BRYCE HARPER, THIS
YEAR'S TOP PROSPECT AND
ONE OF THE MOST HYPED
PLAYERS OF THE DRAFT ERA

FELIX HERNANDEZ, RHP

BIOGRAPHY

PROPER NAME: Felix Abraham Hernandez. **BORN:** April 8, 1986 in Valencia, Venezuela.
HT: 6-3. **WT:** 225. **BATS:** R. **THROWS:** R. **SCHOOL:** U.E. Jose Austre, Valencia, Venezuela.
FIRST PRO CONTRACT: Signed as international free agent by Mariners, July 4, 2002.

TEXAS LEAGUE TOP 10 PROSPECTS FOR 2004

Hernandez showed why he's probably the best pitching prospect in the game, consistently dealing the kind of dominating stuff that invites comparisons to the early version of Dwight Gooden.

With excellent size and body control, Hernandez generally puts his lively, 96-97 mph fastball wherever he wants. He could add velocity as he refines his already sound mechanics and matures physically.

"To see an 18-year-old with that kind of stuff come in and dominate was very impressive," El Paso manager Scott Coolbaugh said. "There was nobody else throwing like him in the league."

— John Manuel

PACIFIC COAST LEAGUE TOP 10 PROSPECTS FOR 2005

King Felix reigned over the PCL with stuff that borders on unfair. His mid-90s fastball and mid-80s curveball are 70 pitches on the 20-80 scouting scale, while his changeup is a 60. The Mariners don't allow him to throw a slider that might be his best pitch—they want to protect his arm and he hasn't needed it—though he'll mix it in occasionally.

Unlike most power pitchers, Hernandez is a groundball machine. He gave up just 14 homers in 306 minor league innings, and big leaguers didn't have any success lifting his pitches either. He throws quality strikes with a sound delivery and clean arm action.

"He's the best minor league pitcher I've ever seen," one scout said. "That's the best report I've ever written."

— Jim Callis

MINOR LEAGUE MENTIONS BY BA

YEAR	TOP 100	ORG RANKING	LEAGUE RANKING	BEST TOOLS
2003			**No. 1:** Northwest	
2004	No. 30	**No. 1:** Mariners	**No. 1:** California **No. 1:** Texas	**CAL:** Best Pitching Prospect, Best Fastball, Best Breaking Pitch
2005	No. 2	**No. 1:** Mariners	**No. 1:** Pacific Coast	**PCL:** Best Pitching Prospect, Best Fastball, Best Breaking Pitch

BaseBall america

MAJORS • MINORS • PROSPECTS • DRAFT • COLLEGE • HIGH SCHOOL

MINOR LEAGUE PREVIEW

Mariners phenom
Felix Hernandez is
the best pitcher
in the minors—but
how long will he
be there?

Angels Move To
The Top Of Our
Minor League
Talent Rankings

LogoMania
Returns!
Check Out The
Best And Worst
Of The Minors

Analysis Of The
Minor League
Talent In Every
Organization

One Man's
Dream To Bring
Professional
Baseball Back
To Mississippi

Pirates
Pitcher
Bryan
Bullington
Heads Into
Pivotal Season

TREVOR HOFFMAN, RHP

BIOGRAPHY

PROPER NAME: Trevor William Hoffman. **BORN:** October 13, 1967 in Bellflower, Calif.
HT: 6-0. **WT:** 220. **BATS:** R. **THROWS:** R. **SCHOOL:** Arizona.
FIRST PRO CONTRACT: Selected by the Reds in 11th round (290th overall) of 1989 draft;
signed June 9, 1989.

CINCINNATI REDS TOP 10 PROSPECTS FOR 1992

A career .227 hitter, Hoffman was on the verge of being released by the Reds after the 1990 season. He was spared only by Jim Lett, his manager at Charleston, who suggested that Hoffman be given one last chance—as a pitcher. Voila! Hoffman always had terrific arm strength, but the Reds never envisioned he would adapt to pitching almost overnight.

He showed rare command for someone who hadn't pitched in years, consistently throwing first-pitch strikes and dominating hitters at Cedar Rapids with a fastball clocked up to 95 mph. Hoffman has progressed so fast that some in the organization believe he has a chance to crack the big league staff in a setup role out of spring training.

— **Allan Simpson**

TOP 10 LONGSHOT PROSPECTS FOR 1992

A shortstop with a weak bat, Hoffman turned to pitching last year as a last resort. It turned out that he had an outstanding fastball that was good enough for 20 saves last year, and possibly a role as a setup man in Cincinnati in 1992.

— **Jim Callis**

MINOR LEAGUE MENTIONS BY BA

YEAR	TOP 100	ORG RANKING	LEAGUE RANKING	BEST TOOLS
1992		**No. 8:** Reds		

TIM HUDSON, RHP

BIOGRAPHY

PROPER NAME: Timothy Adam Hudson. **BORN:** July 14, 1975 in Columbus, Ga.
HT: 6-1. **WT:** 175. **BATS:** R. **THROWS:** R. **SCHOOL:** Auburn.
FIRST PRO CONTRACT: Selected by Athletics in sixth round (185th overall) of 1997 draft;
signed June 13, 1997.

OAKLAND ATHLETICS TOP 10 PROSPECTS FOR 1999

BACKGROUND: Hudson was a two-way star at Auburn, earning a spot on the All-America team as a utilityman his senior season after going 15-2, 2.97 on the mound and batting .396 with 18 home runs and 95 RBIs as a center fielder. He put his bat away when he was drafted by the A's as a pitcher.

STRENGTHS: Around the A's front office, they call Hudson's fastball Super Sink. Not only does it drop, it darts as well. He knows how to use the pitch to induce a lot of ground balls. He also throws an excellent changeup, a satisfactory splitter and an occasional slider.

WEAKNESSES: Hudson is so skinny he can hide behind a fungo bat. The A's worry that he may lack stamina to endure the rigors of a full big league season. The slider also needs work and is not yet of major league caliber.

FUTURE: Hudson has a shot at a major league bullpen job this spring. If the A's decide to leave him as a starter, he will go to Midland or Vancouver.

— **Casey Tefertiller**

PACIFIC COAST LEAGUE TOP TOP 10 PROSPECTS FOR 1999

Hudson shot up the ladder after going 10-9, 4.54 in Double-A last season in his first full pro season. He started back in Double-A and went 3-0, 0.50 before earning promotions to Triple-A and the majors, where he excelled.

"His stuff is electric," said Vancouver manager Mike Quade. "I don't think even our scouting director knew how good he was going to be so quickly."

The only thing the Athletics might need to do to help Hudson's development would be to increase his meal money. He's still pretty skinny.

— **Peter Barrouquere and Laurence Miedema**

MINOR LEAGUE MENTIONS BY BA

YEAR	TOP 100	ORG RANKING	LEAGUE RANKING	BEST TOOLS
1999		No. 10: Athletics	No. 7: Pacific Coast	

DEREK JETER, SS

PROPER NAME: Derek Sanderson Jeter. **BORN:** June 26, 1974 in Pequannock, N.J. **HT:** 6-3. **WT:** 195. **BATS:** R. **THROWS:** R. **SCHOOL:** Kalamazoo (Mich.) Central HS. **FIRST PRO CONTRACT:** Selected by Yankees in first round (sixth overall) of 1992 draft; signed June 27, 1992.

1994 MiLB PLAYER OF THE YEAR

SOUTH ATLANTIC LEAGUE TOP 10 PROSPECTS FOR 1993

He's not Chipper Jones, but Jeter did nothing to discourage supporters. The first high school player drafted in 1992 made a run at the SAL batting title before finishing 11th. He also showed flashes of power and speed.

Jeter was spectacular at times on defense, and managers voted his arm the league's best infield arm in a midseason survey. Consistency is his main need.

"Eventually he's going to hit for power to go with average," Hagerstown manager Jim Nettles said. "He can run. Obviously, they worked with him a lot on defense because he was much better in the second half."

— **Gene Sapakoff**

NEW YORK YANKEES TOP 10 PROSPECTS FOR 1996

BACKGROUND: Jeter didn't electrify baseball in 1995 as he did in 1994, when he was named BA's Minor League Player of the Year. At 20, he was challenged with a full year at Triple-A and led Yankees minor leaguers in hitting.

STRENGTHS: Jeter has the best pure hitting skills in the organization, good strike-zone judgement, sound baserunning instincts and leadership qualities.

WEAKNESSES: Jeter committed 29 errors in 1995, but scouts have difficulty identifying any flaws defensively. He needs subtle refinement in his footwork, but it's not something a steady diet of ground balls and experience won't cure.

FUTURE: Joe Torre has declared Jeter his starting shortstop to start 1996.

— **Allan Simpson**

MINOR LEAGUE MENTIONS BY BA

YEAR	TOP 100	ORG RANKING	LEAGUE RANKING	BEST TOOLS
1993	No. 44	**No. 2:** Yankees	**No. 2:** South Atlantic	**SAL:** Best Defensive SS, Best INF Arm, Most Exciting Player
1994	No. 16	**No. 1:** Yankees	**No. 1:** Florida State **No. 3:** Eastern	**FSL:** Best Hitter, Best INF Arm, Most Exciting Player
1995	No. 4	**No. 2:** Yankees	**No. 3:** International	**IL:** Best Hitter, Most Exciting Player
1996	No. 6	**No. 2:** Yankees		

BaseBall america

PRIDE
OF THE
YANKEES

DEREK JETER:
MINOR LEAGUE
PLAYER OF THE YEAR

RANDY JOHNSON, LHP

BIOGRAPHY

PROPER NAME: Randall David Johnson. **BORN:** September 10, 1963 in Walnut Creek, Ga.
HT: 6-10. **WT:** 225. **BATS:** R. **THROWS:** L. **SCHOOL:** Southern California.
FIRST PRO CONTRACT: Selected by Montreal Expos in second round (36th overall) of 1985
draft; signed June 9, 1985.

FLORIDA STATE LEAGUE TOP 10 PROSPECTS FOR 1986

A 6-foot-10 lefthander who has had his fastball timed as high as 97 mph, Johnson is expected to move up fast in the Expos' system.

West Palm Beach pitching coach Bud Yanus said Johnson, drafted in the second round a year ago out of the University of Southern California, could be in the big leagues inside of two years. "He's got a very good fastball and as long as he stays healthy, he's got a real good chance."

Johnson's biggest obstacle has been his control. He struck out 133 in 119 innings, but allowed 94 bases on balls. But Yanus and Johnson both said that improved mechanics led to better control before the end of the season.

"He used to walk himself right out of games," Expos manager Felipe Alou said. "Now that he has better control, he's doing really well."

— **Randy Rorrer**

AMERICAN ASSOCIATION TOP 10 PROSPECTS FOR 1988

The 6-foot-10 former University of Southern California pitcher has a fastball that peaks at 98 mph. He also seems to be conquering his control problems, though he had to sit out six weeks with a self-inflicted hand injury.

"He'll be a good, solid major league pitcher," said Indianapolis manager Joe Sparks. "He has made great strides mentally and is gaining confidence."

— **George Rorrer**

MINOR LEAGUE MENTIONS BY BA

YEAR	TOP 100	ORG RANKING	LEAGUE RANKING	BEST TOOLS
1986			No. 3: Florida State	FSL: Best Pitching Prospect, Best Fastball
1987		No. 3: Expos	No. 2: Southern	SL: Best Pitching Prospect, Best Fastball
1988		No. 1: Expos	No. 3: American Association	
1989		No. 2: Expos		

ANDRUW JONES, OF

BIOGRAPHY

PROPER NAME: Andruw Rudolf Jones. **BORN:** April 23, 1977 in Willemstad, Curacao. **HT:** 6-1. **WT:** 225. **BATS:** R. **THROWS:** R. **SCHOOL:** St. Paulus, Willemstad, Curacao **FIRST PRO CONTRACT:** Signed as international free agent by Braves, July 1, 1993.

1995 & 1996 MiLB PLAYER OF THE YEAR

ATLANTA BRAVES TOP 10 PROSPECTS FOR 1996

BACKGROUND: BA's 1995 Minor League Player of the Year, Jones was 17 when he started the 1995 season—young even by South Atlantic League standards. But he still dominated the loop and earned recognition from managers as the top prospect. The Curacao native also was named the league's best batting prospect, best power prospect, best baserunner and best defensive outfielder.

STRENGTHS: Jones is the quintessential five-tool talent. One of the most physically mature 18-year-olds scouts have seen, Jones doesn't seem overwhelmed by the game. He makes adjustments between pitches and can hit practically any fastball sent his way. He also has a plus arm and goes into the gaps aggressively. His all-out style and array of talents have drawn comparisons to a young Cesar Cedeno, one of the best teenage players of the last 30 years.

WEAKNESSES: Despite what his 56 stolen bases might indicate, Jones' running ability rates as average. His tremendous quickness makes up for a lack of world-class speed. Jones needs to become more patient at the plate and can't allow his rapid success to go to his head.

FUTURE: Jones is the type of player who can explode through an organization. Several scouts believe he could have succeeded with few problems at Double-A Greenville in 1995. Nevertheless, the Braves want to make sure Jones receives the proper maturing at every step before promoting him.

— **Bill Ballew**

MINOR LEAGUE MENTIONS BY BA

YEAR	TOP 100	ORG RANKING	LEAGUE RANKING	BEST TOOLS
1994			**No. 3:** Gulf Coast **No. 2:** Appalachian	
1995	No. 21	**No. 2:** Braves	**No. 1:** South Atlantic	**SAL:** Best Hitter, Best Power, Best Baserunner, Best Defensive OF, Most Exciting Player
1996	No. 1	**No. 1:** Braves	**No. 1:** Carolina **No. 1:** Southern	**CAR:** Best Hitter, Best Defensive OF, Most Exciting Player
1997	No. 1	**No. 1:** Braves		

CHIPPER JONES, 3B

BIOGRAPHY

PROPER NAME: Larry Wayne Jones. **BORN:** April 24, 1972 in DeLand, Fla.
HT: 6-4. **WT:** 210. **BATS:** B. **THROWS:** R. **SCHOOL:** Bolles HS, Jacksonville.
FIRST PRO CONTRACT: Selected by Braves in first round (first overall) of 1990 draft;
signed June 4, 1990.

SOUTH ATLANTIC LEAGUE TOP 10 PROSPECTS FOR 1991

Larry Wayne Jones smothered a shaky 1990 Gulf Coast League debut (.229, 1 HR, 18 RBIs) with a rousing romp through the SAL (.323, 15 HR, 98 RBIs). What's more, he switch-hit for the first full year of his life.

Erratic at times on defense, Jones, 19, is projected by some as a third baseman. There's no doubt about his arm strength, and he has good range.

"You can see he is a big leaguer biding his time in the minors," a Southern Division manager said. "He got much better in the second half."

— Gene Sapakoff

SOUTHERN LEAGUE TOP 10 PROSPECTS FOR 1992

Jones, a multi-talented switch-hitter, didn't join Greenville until the middle of the season from Class A Durham, but he made a big and lasting impression with his bat. He also was named the No. 1 prospect in the Carolina League.

"He gets better every year," Carolina manager Don Werner said. "I hear a lot of people question his ability to play short in the big leagues, but I've seen him in Macon and in Greenville, and he's really improved."

Greenville manager Grady Little said Jones is something special: "I think the Braves are fortunate to have him in their organization. He's a person a lot of people will get enjoyment from, and it has nothing to do with what he does on the field. He's got a lot of charisma."

— Rubin Grant

MINOR LEAGUE MENTIONS BY BA

YEAR	TOP 100	ORG RANKING	LEAGUE RANKING	BEST TOOLS
1991	No. 49	**No. 2:** Braves	**No. 2:** South Atlantic	**SAL:** Best Infield Arm
1992	No. 4	**No. 1:** Braves	**No. 1:** Carolina **No. 1:** Southern	**CAR:** Best Defensive SS
1993	No. 1	**No. 1:** Braves	**No. 2:** International	
1994	No. 2	**No. 1:** Braves		
1995	No. 3	**No. 1:** Braves		

JEFF KENT, 2B

BIOGRAPHY

PROPER NAME: Jeffrey Franklin Kent. **BORN:** March 7, 1968 in Bellflower, Calif.
HT: 6-2. **WT:** 210. **BATS:** R. **THROWS:** R. **SCHOOL:** California.
FIRST PRO CONTRACT: Selected by Blue Jays in 20th round (523rd overall) of 1989 draft;
signed June 9, 1989.

TORONTO BLUE JAYS ORG. REPORT, MAY 1992

Jeff Kent wasn't surprised when he was sent to Triple-A at the end of spring training. He wasn't disappointed. He understood.

"I've got a smile on my face and I'm going to go down and work hard," he said. Kent made an impression during spring training when he batted .375.

Converted from a shortstop-third baseman to second base in 1990, Kent also showed a strong arm when he had a chance to play third in exhibition games. He didn't have to wait long for his call to the majors, as injuries meant Kent was called up two games into the major league season.

"I'm probably the most expendable player on this team" Kent said. "I won't be regretful if I am sent down. That's my role right now. But you never know."

His comments proved prophetic. The Jays may be regretful if the time comes to return Kent to Syracuse. When Kelly Gruber begged off with neck spasms against the Orioles, Kent took his place. In his first at-bat, he doubled. In his second at-bat, he hit the ball even harder but right at the third baseman.

As Gruber rested his neck, Kent had at least one hit in each of his first three games, including his first big league homer in a 12-6 rout of the Yankees.

Fans were beginning to wonder if Kent could play shortstop instead of the light-hitting Manuel Lee. Kent, who played shortstop at California says former Blue Jays infielder Garth Iorg, who coached at Class A Dunedin before managing at Rookie-level Medicine Hat, helped his conversion to second base.

"I respect him a lot," Kent said. "I never had a chance to play for him, but as a coach that half-season at Dunedin he taught me a lot about the mental part of the game. We're both Mormons. That doesn't mean everything in the world, but we respect each other because of that."

— **Larry Millson**

MINOR LEAGUE MENTIONS BY BA

YEAR	TOP 100	ORG RANKING	LEAGUE RANKING	BEST TOOLS
1990				**FSL:** Best Defensive 2B

CLAYTON KERSHAW, LHP

BIOGRAPHY

PROPER NAME: Clayton Edward Kershaw. **BORN:** March 19, 1988 in Dallas, Texas.
HT: 6-4. **WT:** 228. **BATS:** L. **THROWS:** L. **SCHOOL:** Highland Park HS, University Park, Texas.
FIRST PRO CONTRACT: Selected by Dodgers in first round (seventh overall) of 2006 draft; signed June 20, 2006.

GULF COAST LEAGUE TOP 10 PROSPECTS FOR 2006

Kershaw established himself as the best high school prospect in the 2006 draft when he dominated Texas high school competition. The Dodgers signed him for $2.3 million and let him spend his summer in the GCL.

He maintained his stuff throughout the season, regularly showing a fastball that sat between 90-94 mph and touched 96, as well as a plus curveball. His changeup is solid average and has the makings of a dependable third offering.

"He has a good sense of how to pitch and he competes well," Dodgers manager Juan Bustabad said. "He goes right after the hitters and as soon as he got his first start, he was overpowering. He's going to move up fast."

— Alan Matthews

MIDWEST LEAGUE TOP 10 PROSPECTS FOR 2007

The Dodgers handled Kershaw carefully in 2006 after drafting him seventh overall, then took the gloves off this year. After he blew away MWL hitters, they jumped him to Double-A and he had little trouble against older hitters.

Of course, it's easy to succeed with two swing-and-miss pitches. Kershaw had the best fastball in the league as well as one of the best curveballs. No minor league lefty can match his power stuff. His changeup could give him a third plus pitch, though he had little need for it until he got to Double-A.

"He was by far the highest-ceiling minor league arm I saw all year. The second-best was Clay Buchholz," a National League scout said. "Kershaw could end up winning Cy Young Awards. Not many young guys do what he does."

— Jim Callis

MINOR LEAGUE MENTIONS BY BA

YEAR	TOP 100	ORG RANKING	LEAGUE RANKING	BEST TOOLS
2006			**No. 1:** Gulf Coast	
2007	No. 24	**No. 2:** Dodgers	**No. 1:** Midwest	**MWL:** Best Pitching Prospect, Best Fastball
2008	No. 7	**No. 1:** Dodgers	**No. 1:** Southern	**SL:** Best Pitching Prospect, Best Fastball, Best Breaking Pitch

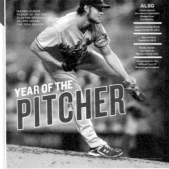

DALLAS KEUCHEL, LHP

BIOGRAPHY

PROPER NAME: Dallas Keuchel. **BORN:** January 1, 1988 in Tulsa, Okla.
HT: 6-3. **WT:** 205. **BATS:** L. **THROWS:** L. **SCHOOL:** Arkansas.
FIRST PRO CONTRACT: Selected by Astros in seventh round (221st overall) of 2009 draft;
signed June 24, 2009.

HOUSTON ASTROS TOP 30 PROSPECTS FOR 2011

Keuchel's pedigree suggests he would rank much higher on this list. He was a Friday starter in the Southeastern Conference at Arkansas and enough of an athlete to be recruited as a quarterback by his hometown college, Tulsa. But he doesn't have the pure stuff to rate as a premium prospect.

Keuchel had a successful 2010 season, leading the organization with 174 innings and reaching Double-A. He generates impressive sink on his fastball and changeup, and he gave up just 10 home runs in the hitter-friendly California League—with eight in 58 innings at Lancaster's unforgiving park. His 1.9 walks per nine innings ratio adds to his appeal.

The problem is that his fastball has lost velocity since college. He sat at 86-91 mph and touched 93 mph for the Razorbacks, but his delivery has become stiffer and more mechanical since signing, and he worked at 83-86 mph in 2010.

Keuchel's curveball has been a swing-and-miss pitch at lower levels because he locates it well, but scouts consider it fringy because it breaks early.

If he regains velocity and arm speed by improving his tempo and delivery, he should fit at the back of a big league rotation. It's hard to see him continuing to have success otherwise, so the Astros hope his velocity bounces back when he returns to Corpus Christi to start 2011.

— **John Manuel**

MINOR LEAGUE MENTIONS BY BA

YEAR	TOP 100	ORG RANKING	LEAGUE RANKING	BEST TOOLS
2010		No. 24: Astros		CAR: Best Changeup
2011		No. 23: Astros		TL: Best Changeup
2012		No. 21: Astros		

JUSTIN K. ALLER/GETTY IMAGES

CRAIG KIMBREL, RHP

BIOGRAPHY

PROPER NAME: Craig Michael Kimbrel. **BORN:** May 28, 1988 in Huntsville, Ala.
HT: 6-0. **WT:** 210. **BATS:** R. **THROWS:** R. **SCHOOL:** Wallace State (Ala.) JC.
FIRST PRO CONTRACT: Selected by Braves in third round (96th overall) of 2008 draft;
signed June 6, 2008.

ATLANTA BRAVES TOP 10 PROSPECTS FOR 2011

The Braves selected 10 junior college players in the first 15 rounds of the 2008 draft, starting with Kimbrel in the third round. He signed for $391,000 after turning down $125,000 from Atlanta as a 33rd-round pick a year earlier.

He ranked third in the International League with 23 saves and reached the big leagues in his second full pro season. He was dynamic during the pennant race, finishing the year with 12 scoreless big league outings while striking out 23 batters in 12 innings.

Kimbrel has averaged 14.8 strikeouts per nine innings as a pro, thanks to his heavy fastball, which sits at 93-96 mph with excellent sink. His slurvy curveball gives him a second plus pitch to complement his heater. After rarely throwing a changeup in 2009, he worked on the pitch prior to last season and mixed it in on occasion.

While moving faster than anticipated, Kimbrel has made significant strides with his command and his ability to pitch inside. Reminiscent of a righthanded Billy Wagner, he has the stuff and makeup to finish games.

The Braves tried to expose Kimbrel to the job of a major league closer and Wagner's expertise without rushing him in 2010. He responded well, putting himself in position to take over as Atlanta's closer in 2011 following Wagner's retirement.

— **Bill Ballew**

MINOR LEAGUE MENTIONS BY BA

YEAR	TOP 100	ORG RANKING	LEAGUE RANKING	BEST TOOLS
2008			No. 14: Appalachian	
2009		No. 10: Braves		CAR: Best Fastball
2010		No. 5: Braves		
2011	No. 86	No. 5: Braves		

COREY KLUBER, RHP

BIOGRAPHY

PROPER NAME: Corey Scott Kluber. **BORN:** April 10, 1986 in Birmingham, Ala.
HT: 6-4. **WT:** 215. **BATS:** R. **THROWS:** R. **SCHOOL:** Stetson.
FIRST PRO CONTRACT: Selected by Padres in fourth round (134th overall) of 2007 draft;
signed July 17, 2007.

SAN DIEGO PADRES TOP 30 PROSPECTS FOR 2008

After a stress fracture in his throwing arm in high school required surgery and the insertion of a screw that remains in his arm, Kluber developed into a reliable starter for Stetson. The 2007 Atlantic Sun Conference pitcher of the year after going 12-2, 2.05, he signed with the Padres for $200,000.

At 6-foot-4 and 215 pounds, Kluber pounds the zone with three pitches. He pitches at 88-92 mph, touching 94 mph with above-average life, and he holds his velocity late in outings. His slider and changeup are average at times.

Though Kluber lacks a put-away pitch, he reads swings well and understands how to attack batters. Kluber could develop into a No. 4 starter in time.

— **Ben Badler**

INTERNATIONAL LEAGUE TOP 20 PROSPECTS FOR 2012

The IL's lack of power arms made Kluber stand out in comparison despite his age. The durable 26-year-old shaved nearly two runs off his ERA at Columbus in 2011, though he was hit hard in his first extended big league stint.

Kluber shows flashes of dominance thanks to a fastball that sits at 92-94 and touches 95. He gets in trouble when his fastball flattens out, which happens more than it should for a pitcher his size. His slider is his best pitch, peaking at 86 and flashing good depth, and his changeup can be a solid offering.

"His changeup was not a pitch he could go to in 2011. It was this year," [Columbus manager Mike] Sarbaugh said. "The issue for him is fastball command, it all comes down to that. He has to be finer with his fastball because he's shown the ability to get swings and misses with the fastball and slider."

— **Ben Badler**

MINOR LEAGUE MENTIONS BY BA

YEAR	TOP 100	ORG RANKING	LEAGUE RANKING	BEST TOOLS
2008		No. 29: Padres		
2011		No. 26: Indians		
2012			No. 12: International	IL: Best Breaking Pitch

BARRY LARKIN, SS

BIOGRAPHY

PROPER NAME: Barry Louis Larkin. **BORN:** April 28, 1964 in Cincinnati.
HT: 6-0. **WT:** 185. **BATS:** R. **THROWS:** R. **SCHOOL:** Michigan.
FIRST PRO CONTRACT: Selected by Reds in first round (fourth overall) of 1985 draft;
signed June 3, 1985.

TOP COLLEGE PROSPECTS FOR 1985 DRAFT

A former football standout at Cincinnati's famed Moeller High School, Larkin has elected to pursue baseball only at Michigan. While scouts are in general agreement that he's the best shortstop prospect in the country, he's not mechanically sound yet—largely because of his Northern background.

"He hasn't regressed at all since high school," said one scouting director. "And with a lack of infielders in the draft this year, you might see some over-drafting at shortstop, which wouldn't hurt Larkin."

— **Allan Simpson**

CINCINNATI REDS TOP 10 PROSPECTS FOR 1986

When Larkin came out of Cincinnati's Moeller High School in 1982, the Reds thought enough of him to make him a second-round selection. Larkin, however, turned them down and decided to go to the University of Michigan.

The Reds never gave up hope, and when Larkin was eligible in the draft again last summer, they used their No. 1 pick to take him. This time he signed, and he gave the Reds nothing but reason for optimism with his debut.

Larkin looked right at home in Double-A, hitting .267 for Vermont. He didn't show power (one home run in 255 at-bats), but that will come. They key for him was just getting his feet on the ground, and he was not overpowered by the high level of competition. He will have good power for a shortstop. In fact, he should hit enough that he could be moved to third base.

It would only be because of [Kurt] Stillwell that Larkin would have to change positions. He's got the range and natural actions of a shortstop and good enough arm strength to play the position on turf.

— **Tracy Ringolsby**

MINOR LEAGUE MENTIONS BY BA

YEAR	TOP 100	ORG RANKING	LEAGUE RANKING	BEST TOOLS
1986		**No. 8:** Reds	**No. 2:** American Association	**AA:** Best Defensive SS

Major League Organization Reports
Minor League Previews
Atlanta Has Baseball's Best Farm Set-Up

ROLLS ROYCE
San Francisco's
Roger Clayton
Exudes Confidence

Baseball america

APRIL 21 - MAY 5, 1987   YOU CAN'T GET ANYWHERE ELSE $2.25 ($2.75 CANADA)

KING OF THE QUEEN CITY

Barry Larkin Sparks
For His Hometown
Cincinnati Reds

Little Brother Strikes,
A University Of Texas
Outfielder, Chases
The Same Dream

THE BEST PROSPECTS
AROUND THE WORLD

VENERABLE
VENEZUELANS:
WILSON ALVAREZ,
RICH GARCES

ARIZONA STATE
COACH JIM BROCK
REACHES A MILESTONE

OCEAN VIEW HIGH'S
INTRIGUING
CLASS OF 1987

CLIFF LEE, LHP

BIOGRAPHY

PROPER NAME: Clifton Phifer Lee. **BORN:** August 30, 1978 in Benton, Ark.
HT: 6-3. **WT:** 205. **BATS:** L. **THROWS:** L. **SCHOOL:** Benton (Ark.) HS.
FIRST PRO CONTRACT: Selected by Montreal Expos in fourth round (105th overall) of 2000 draft; signed July 6, 2000.

EASTERN LEAGUE TOP 10 PROSPECTS FOR 2002

Another key component to the [Bartolo] Colon trade, Lee got a higher profile when he changed organizations. He was the EL's runaway leader in strikeouts before he was promoted to Triple-A in mid-July.

Lee attacks hitters with a varied arsenal that includes two- and four-seam fastballs, a slider, a curveball and a changeup. He doesn't throw exceptionally hard, usually pitching around 90 mph with his sinker, but he's difficult to hit because he generates a lot of movement with his pitches.

"He's competitive, he's athletic and he has the potential for four outstanding pitches," an NL scout said. "If he keeps getting command, he might even have ace potential at the major league level."

— **Andrew Linker**

CLEVELAND INDIANS TOP 10 PROSPECTS FOR 2003

After coming to the Indians in the Colon deal, Lee jumped from Double-A to Triple-A to the big leagues, getting rave reviews at each level. Lee is a rare pitcher who can win without his best stuff. And when he's on, watch out.

His fastball sits at 91-93 mph, his slider has good late action, and his curveball and changeup give hitters something else to worry about. Lee is so smooth that hitters don't get a good read on his pitches until they're halfway to the plate. Lee's velocity was down to the high 80s in September, probably because his innings jumped in 2002.

Lee is a candidate to win one of the openings in the rotation behind C.C. Sabathia. He, Billy Traber and Brian Tallet give Cleveland three advanced southpaws, and Lee has the most upside.

— **Jim Ingraham**

MINOR LEAGUE MENTIONS BY BA

YEAR	TOP 100	ORG RANKING	LEAGUE RANKING	BEST TOOLS
2001		**No. 21:** Expos		
2002		**No. 11:** Expos	**No. 5:** Eastern	**EL:** Best Breaking Pitch
2003	No. 30	**No. 3:** Indians	**No. 8:** International	

BaseBall america

PLUS

Looking At How
General Manager's
Job Has Evolved
Over Last Decade,
Along With List Of
Top GM Prospects

Two Familiar Names
Sit Atop
Our Annual List Of
Top 20 Rookies

Find Out How
Baseball Shares
Its Wealth—And
How Much Wealth
There Is

Get To Know
New Union Leader
Mike Weiner,
A Departure From
Past Leadership

Exclusive
Excerpt From
Dirk Hayhurst's
New Book

Projecting How
Your Favorite Team
Will Perform
This Season

We Take A Look
Back At Major
League Events
In The Aughts

MAJOR
LEAGUE
PREVIEW

General Manager Jack Zduriencik And New Acquisition Cliff Lee Have Seattle Fans Excited

JON LESTER, LHP

BIOGRAPHY

PROPER NAME: Jonathan Tyler Lester. **BORN:** January 7, 1984 in Tacoma.
HT: 6-4. **WT:** 240. **BATS:** L. **THROWS:** L. **SCHOOL:** Bellarmine Prep, Tacoma.
FIRST PRO CONTRACT: Selected by Red Sox in second round (57th overall) of 2002 draft;
signed Aug. 13, 2002.

BOSTON RED SOX TOP 10 PROSPECTS FOR 2006

Lester's long-awaited breakout finally came in 2005, when he was Boston's minor league pitcher of the year. He won the same award in the Double-A Eastern League, which he led in ERA, complete games and strikeouts. He was part of the failed Alex Rodriguez trade talks in 2003, but the Red Sox refused to part with him in the Josh Beckett deal.

Lester is a big, physical lefthander with a chance for three plus pitches. His fastball has late life and has risen from 87-88 mph in 2003 to 90-91 in 2004 to 92-93 last year, when he topped out at 95 mph. He has turned his cut fastball into a true slider that's now his No. 2 pitch. He can get both swings and misses and called strikes with his changeup.

Once Lester gets a little more consistent with his secondary pitches and his command, he'll be ready for the big leagues. He'll keep batters off-balance by throwing an occasional curveball, but it lags behind his other offerings.

Boston doesn't have an opening in its rotation, so Lester will head to Triple-A. He should be ready if needed by the second half, and he has the stuff to become a frontline starter.

— **Jim Callis**

MINOR LEAGUE MENTIONS BY BA

YEAR	TOP 100	ORG RANKING	LEAGUE RANKING	BEST TOOLS
2003		**No. 8:** Red Sox		
2004		**No. 8:** Red Sox	**No. 15:** Florida State	
2005		**No. 4:** Red Sox	**No. 4:** Eastern	
2006	No. 22	**No. 2:** Red Sox		

TIM LINCECUM, RHP

BIOGRAPHY

PROPER NAME: Timothy LeRoy Lincecum. **BORN:** June 15, 1984 in Bellevue, Wash.
HT: 5-11. **WT:** 170. **BATS:** L. **THROWS:** R. **SCHOOL:** Washington.
FIRST PRO CONTRACT: Selected by Giants in first round (10th overall) of 2006 draft;
signed June 30, 2006.

SAN FRANCISCO GIANTS TOP 10 PROSPECTS FOR 2007

When Lincecum was available with the 10th overall pick in the 2006 draft, the Giants felt like they had just won the lottery. After a couple of tuneups with short-season Salem Keizer, Lincecum dominated at high Class A San Jose and struck out 10 over seven innings to win his lone playoff start.

Lincecum throws a 91-96 mph fastball that tops out at 98 mph. If that weren't enough, he also has a true hammer curveball that breaks early and keeps on breaking. Giants scouts believe he might have the best curve of any drafted player since Kerry Wood. He added a changeup during his Cape [Cod League] stint, and at times it's a swing-and-miss pitch that bottoms out at the plate. During the spring, he also unveiled a hard slider that he can throw for strikes.

Lincecum's combination of stuff and deception makes him close to unhittable. He's incredibly strong for a pitcher his size, and some old-timers say he reminds them of Bob Feller or a righthanded Sandy Koufax because of his delivery and flexibility. That's no coincidence, because Lincecum's father watched Koufax pitch and taught his son to copy the Hall of Famer's mechanics.

Lincecum logged 342 innings in his three seasons at Washington, frequently exceeding 120 pitches per start. While he claims to have never felt soreness in his arm, some scouts believe he's a breakdown waiting to happen. He could be the devastating closer the Giants have lacked since Robb Nen injured his shoulder in 2002, but they say Lincecum will be a starter until he proves he can't handle the role. If he dominates, San Francisco will have a hard time keeping him off the Opening Day roster.

— **Andy Baggarly**

MINOR LEAGUE MENTIONS BY BA

YEAR	TOP 100	ORG RANKING	LEAGUE RANKING	BEST TOOLS
2007	No. 11	**No. 1:** Giants		**PCL:** Best Pitching Prospect, Best Fastball, Best Breaking Pitch

FRANCISCO LINDOR, SS

BIOGRAPHY

PROPER NAME: Francisco Miguel Lindor. **BORN:** November 14, 1993 in Caguas, Puerto Rico.
HT: 5-11. **WT:** 190. **BATS:** B. **THROWS:** R. **SCHOOL:** Montverde (Fla.) Academy.
FIRST PRO CONTRACT: Selected by Indians in first round (eighth overall) of 2011 draft;
signed Aug. 15, 2011.

CAROLINA LEAGUE TOP 10 PROSPECTS FOR 2013

One year after playing as the youngest position player in the Midwest League, Lindor spent the first half of 2013 as the second-youngest regular in the Carolina League at age 19. Once again, he looked more like a wily veteran than an overmatched teenager, drawing as much praise for his leadership skills and high baseball IQ as his physical tools.

"He is one of the better defenders at his age that I have seen in a while at shortstop," Frederick manager Ryan Minor said. "His communication and game awareness are advanced."

Lindor can do it all defensively. He has above-average range to both sides, soft hands and a strong arm. He addressed a need by spending considerable time working on improving his backhand with Indians special assistant Travis Fryman, the former big league third baseman.

A switch-hitter, Lindor has a compact swing and barrels the ball from both sides. He ought to hit for high average because he does a good job of taking what pitchers give him. Though not much of a power hitter, Lindor could enhance his home-run output as he fills out and improves his pitch recognition. He's an instinctual basestealer who takes advantage of average speed.

"He puts the barrel on the ball and drives it," Carolina manager David Wallace said. "It wouldn't surprise me to see 15-20 home runs from him."

— **Ben Badler**

MINOR LEAGUE MENTIONS BY BA

YEAR	TOP 100	ORG RANKING	LEAGUE RANKING	BEST TOOLS
2012	No. 37	**No. 1:** Indians	**No. 3:** Midwest	**MWL:** Best Defensive SS
2013	No. 28	**No. 1:** Indians	**No. 1:** Carolina	**CAR:** Best Defensive SS, Most Exciting Player
2014	No. 13	**No. 1:** Indians	**No. 3:** Eastern **No. 3:** International	**EL:** Best Defensive SS, Best INF Arm
2015	No. 19	**No. 1:** Indians	**No. 1:** International	**IL:** Best Defensive SS, Most Exciting Player

INSIDE PUTTING THE GIANTS' WORLD SERIES VICTORY IN PERSPECTIVE

BaseBall america

TOP 10 PROSPECTS

ARIZONA FALL LEAGUE: A CORNUCOPIA OF COVERAGE!

DID PITCHING IN THE MAJORS MAKE BRANDON FINNEGAN THE ROYALS' TOP PROSPECT?

WRAPPING SHOWCASE SEASON: TOP 2015 PROSPECTS SHINE IN JUPITER

FRANCISCO LINDOR RANKS AS CLEVELAND'S NO. 1 PROSPECT FOR THE FOURTH STRAIGHT YEAR

WITH HONORS

KENNY LOFTON, OF

BIOGRAPHY

PROPER NAME: Kenneth Lofton. **BORN:** May 31, 1967 in East Chicago, Ind.
HT: 6-0. **WT:** 180. **BATS:** L. **THROWS:** L. **SCHOOL:** Arizona.
FIRST PRO CONTRACT: Selected by Astros in 17th round (428th overall) of 1988 draft;
signed June 16, 1988.

HOUSTON ASTROS TOP 10 PROSPECTS FOR 1991

Now that he's concentrating solely on baseball, Lofton is on the fast track to Houston. He was the most improved player in the organization in 1990, and should skip Double-A in 1991 and play in Tucson, where he was a basketball player at the University of Arizona.

Lofton is the fastest player in the organization and one of the fastest in the game. He's an exceptional bunter. He's still a little green running the bases, but the Astros have encouraged him to be aggressive and not worry about getting picked off.

Lofton hits with surprising power. He can drive the ball to the opposite field and stands in well against lefthanders. His arm is a little short for center field, and he often takes a poor route in tracking down balls, but he outruns most of his mistakes.

— **Allan Simpson**

PACIFIC COAST LEAGUE TOP 10 PROSPECTS FOR 1991

Pure, raw talent. After making the jump from A ball, Lofton hit .308 with two home runs and 50 RBIs. A former basketball star from the Unviersity of Arizona, he has played only two and a half seasons of professional baseball.

Lofton has great speed in the outfield, and his 28 assists attest to his arm strength. He struck out 95 times in 130 games, but he cut down on his whiffs in the second half. He stole 40 bases in 63 attempts, but again, he was more successful as the season went along.

— **Mike Klis**

MINOR LEAGUE MENTIONS BY BA

YEAR	TOP 100	ORG RANKING	LEAGUE RANKING	BEST TOOLS
1991	No. 75	**No. 4:** Astros	**No. 1:** Pacific Coast	**PCL:** Best Baserunner, Fastest Baserunner, Most Exciting Player
1992	No. 28	**No. 1:** Indians		

SPECIAL BONUS SECTION: Previewing The Olympics

Who Is Jose Pett And Why Did He Cost Toronto $700,000?

Baseball america

AUGUST 10–24, 1992 "BASEBALL NEWS YOU CAN'T GET ANYWHERE ELSE" $2.95 ($3.75 CANADA)

MEN OF STEAL

MONTREAL'S MARQUIS GRISSOM AND CLEVELAND'S KENNY LOFTON
THE NEW GENERATION OF BASE STEALERS

BASEBALL'S BEST TOOLS

MANAGERS IDENTIFY THE BEST TALENTS
IN THE MAJOR AND MINOR LEAGUES
Tom Glavine, National League's Best Pitcher

EVAN LONGORIA, 3B

BIOGRAPHY

PROPER NAME: Evan Michael Longoria. **BORN:** October 7, 1985 in Downey, Calif.
HT: 6-1. **WT:** 215. **BATS:** R. **THROWS:** R. **SCHOOL:** Long Beach State.
FIRST PRO CONTRACT: Selected by Rays in first round (third overall) of 2006 draft;
signed June 7, 2006.

TAMPA BAY RAYS TOP 10 PROSPECTS FOR 2008

Longoria has blistered professional pitching since he unexpectedly fell to the Rays as the third overall pick in the 2006 draft and signed for $3 million.

Longoria displays a great feel for hitting with a disciplined approach and impressive raw power. Both his bat and his power rate as 70 tools on the 20-80 scouting scale. With quick hands and strong wrists, he has a loose and easy swing, producing great leverage and exceptional bat speed.

When Double-A pitchers began to pitch around Longoria last season, he showed improved patience. Even so, he's an aggressive hitter who will swing at any time in the count if he gets his pitch. With his solid pitch recognition, he rarely misses a mistake.

Defensively, Longoria is an above-average third baseman with soft hands and solid body control. His footwork is a plus, both with his lateral movement and with charging the ball on slow rollers. His arm strength is another plus, and his throws have good carry and accuracy.

He competes hard and has good makeup. There are times when Longoria's aggressiveness gets the best of him, particularly when it comes to chasing sliders down and away in the strike zone.

His biggest shortcoming is his speed, which grades as slightly below-average and led to just adequate range at shortstop, prompting his position switch. He does, however, run the bases well with his impressive instincts.

The Rays should have a Rookie of the Year candidate at third base for the second straight season. He has little to prove in the minors and will push Akinori Otsuka to second base when ready. Longoria gives every indication of becoming an All-Star, hitting .300 with 30-plus homers on an annual basis.

— **Bill Ballew**

MINOR LEAGUE MENTIONS BY BA

YEAR	TOP 100	ORG RANKING	LEAGUE RANKING	BEST TOOLS
2007	No. 7	**No. 2:** Rays	**No. 2:** Southern	**SL:** Best Power
2008	No. 2	**No. 1:** Rays		

MANNY MACHADO, 3B

BIOGRAPHY

PROPER NAME: Manuel Arturo Machado. **BORN:** July 6, 1992 in Hialeah, Fla.
HT: 6-3. **WT:** 185. **BATS:** R. **THROWS:** R. **SCHOOL:** Brito Miami Private HS.
FIRST PRO CONTRACT: Selected by Orioles in first round (third overall) of 2010 draft;
signed August 16, 2010.

BALTIMORE ORIOLES TOP 10 PROSPECTS FOR 2011

The Orioles have leaned toward pitching at the top of recent drafts and hadn't selected a shortstop in the first round since taking Rich Dauer out of Southern California in 1974, but Machado's talent was too much to pass up. The scouting consensus was that the top three players in the 2010 draft—Bryce Harper, Jameson Taillon and Machado—were a cut above everyone else, so the Orioles were happy to grab their shortstop of the future with the No. 3 overall choice after the Nationals picked Harper and the Pirates selected Taillon.

The Orioles brought in J.J. Hardy to fill their gaping hole at shortstop, but long term they had no one in the system to take over the position until signing Machado, who has legitimate five-tool ability. He has a good swing and bat speed. He makes consistent hard contact—he struck out just three times in 36 pro at-bats—and repeatedly puts the barrel on the ball. The ball already carries well off his bat, and he has the room to add muscle to his wiry 6-foot-3 frame.

Machado also has the arm, build and strength to be a major league short-stop. He shows advanced defensive skills, with solid range, soft hands and a plus arm. His weakest tool is his speed, but even that rates as fringe-average. In addition to his physical ability, Machado has made a quick impression with his makeup, showing a great work ethic and receptiveness to instruction.

Because of his build, Dominican bloodlines and hype as a high school shortstop coming out of South Florida, he earns obvious Alex Rodriguez comparisons. He's not as physically mature as Rodriguez was when he came into pro ball, and his ceiling isn't as lofty, but Machado still has the look of a perennial All-Star.

— **Will Lingo**

MINOR LEAGUE MENTIONS BY BA

YEAR	TOP 100	ORG RANKING	LEAGUE RANKING	BEST TOOLS
2011	No. 14	**No. 1:** Orioles	**No. 2:** South Atlantic **No. 1:** Carolina	
2012	No. 11	**No. 2:** Orioles	**No. 1:** Eastern	**EL:** Best Defensive SS, Best INF Arm, Most Exciting Player

GREG MADDUX, RHP

BIOGRAPHY

PROPER NAME: Gregory Alan Maddux. **BORN:** April 14, 1966 in San Angelo, Texas.
HT: 6-0. **WT:** 195. **BATS:** R. **THROWS:** R. **SCHOOL:** Valley HS, Las Vegas.
FIRST PRO CONTRACT: Selected by Cubs in second round of 1984 draft; signed June 19, 1984.

MIDWEST LEAGUE TOP 10 PROSPECTS FOR 1985

He's only 19, but he's still got a major league arm—an 88 mph fastball and good control. Now, Maddux needs to develop a consistent curve.

"For his age, he's got an excellent fastball," Appleton manager Sal Rende said. "He's got a decent breaking pitch, but [the Cubs] need to take their time with him so he can learn how to pitch."

Maddux was praised for his poise and was voted the league's best pitching prospect in a midseason poll. But some managers questioned whether the 6-foot, 150-pounder was strong enough to make it to the majors.

"When he learns to control that curve he's going to move up as fast as anyone can move," Peoria manager Pete Mackanin said. "He's going to be a major league pitcher."

— **Jon Scher**

CHICAGO CUBS TOP 10 PROSPECTS FOR 1986

Despite his slight build, Maddux throws an above-average fastball that moves well, and he has a power curve when he doesn't rush his delivery. He had a good season at Peoria (13-9, 3.19, 125 strikeouts and 52 walks in 186 innings), although physical fatigue took a toll in the final month.

The Cubs think he will get bigger and stronger. Mike Maddux, an older brother who pitches in the Phillies' system, was about the same size at the same age but has grown to 6-foot-2, 180 pounds.

— **Ken Leiker**

MINOR LEAGUE MENTIONS BY BA

YEAR	TOP 100	ORG RANKING	LEAGUE RANKING	BEST TOOLS
1984			**No. 4:** Appalachian	
1985		**No. 5:** Cubs	**No. 3:** Midwest	**MWL:** Best Pitching Prospect
1986		**No. 7:** Cubs	**No. 6:** American Association	
1987		**No. 5:** Cubs		

RUSSELL MARTIN, C

BIOGRAPHY

PROPER NAME: Russell Nathan Coltrane Martin. **BORN:** February 15, 1983 in East York, Canada.
HT: 5-10. **WT:** 205. **BATS:** R. **THROWS:** R. **SCHOOL:** Chipola (Fla.) JC.
FIRST PRO CONTRACT: Selected by Dodgers in 17th round (511th overall) of 2002 draft;
signed June 13, 2002.

LOS ANGELES DODGERS TOP 10 PROSPECTS FOR 2005

Outside of Joel Guzman, Martin made the most significant leap in the system last year. A 35th-round pick by the Expos out of Montreal ABC baseball Academy in 2000, he played two years at Chipola (Fla.) JC before signing with the Dodgers for $40,000. He moved from third base to catcher in 2003.

Martin made strides in his defensive game last year. He's quick, uses his excellent footwork to help him block balls in the dirt and has a well above-average arm. Offensively, he has a line-drive stroke, good plate discipline and the potential to hit 15-20 homers annually. He's durable, works hard and has a strong makeup. He needs to maintain his focus throughout games, but more than anything else he requires more experience behind the plate.

Martin will open the season in Double-A. He has no challenger as the Dodgers' catcher of the future and may be ready for the majors by Sept. 2006.

— **Alan Matthews**

SOUTHERN LEAGUE TOP 10 PROSPECTS FOR 2005

With [Brian] McCann in Atlanta, Martin might be the best catcher left in the minors. Converted from third base in 2003, he has the complete package, right down to his ability to steal an occasional base. His strike-zone judgment is exquisite, and he hits for average to all fields with power to the gaps.

An intense player with strong leadership skills, Martin calls a good game, handles pitchers well and always backs up bases. His catch-and-throw skills are outstanding. He can get better at blocking, but he has made a lot of progress.

— **Aaron Fitt**

MINOR LEAGUE MENTIONS BY BA

YEAR	TOP 100	ORG RANKING	LEAGUE RANKING	BEST TOOLS
2004		**No. 18:** Dodgers		
2005	No. 89	**No. 6:** Dodgers	**No. 10:** Southern	**SL:** Best Strike-Zone Judgment, Best Defensive C
2006	No. 42	**No. 4:** Dodgers		

EDGAR MARTINEZ, DH

BIOGRAPHY

PROPER NAME: Edgar Martinez. **BORN:** January 2, 1963 in New York, N.Y.
HT: 5-11. **WT:** 210. **BATS:** R. **THROWS:** R. **SCHOOL:** American College, Puerto Rico.
FIRST PRO CONTRACT: Signed as international free agent by Mariners, Dec. 19, 1982.

SEATTLE MARINERS TOP 10 PROSPECTS FOR 1985

What a difference a year made for Martinez. After being signed out of Puerto Rico in 1982, he debuted at Bellingham and there was little hope for his development. He hit a weak .173. During the offseason, however, he matured physically and came back last summer much stronger.

The 300-foot fly ball outs suddenly went 350 feet, and the ground balls in the hole went through the hole. He drove the ball and hit for average at Wausau (.303, 32 doubles, 15 HR, 66 RBIs). If he continues to develop with the bat, he can play third base. He has average speed, good reactions and a good arm.

— **Tracy Ringolsby**

SEATTLE MARINERS TOP 10 PROSPECTS FOR 1989

One reason that Jim Presley's name kept popping up in trade rumors is the development of Martinez, signed as a free agent out of Puerto Rico in 1982. After two years at Triple-A—including leading all minor leaguers with a .363 average last year—he's got nothing to prove at any level below the big leagues.

Martinez doesn't have the pure power of his cousin, Carmelo, but he is a pure hitter. He has a composite .342 average the last two years, achieved by driving the ball to all fields. Martinez doesn't give pitchers any breaks. In five full professional seasons, he's walked 410 times and struck out only 228 times.

Martinez has the soft hands of a middle infielder, the quick step of a third baseman and a solid throwing arm.

— **Tracy Ringolsby**

MINOR LEAGUE MENTIONS BY BA

YEAR	TOP 100	ORG RANKING	LEAGUE RANKING	BEST TOOLS
1985		**No. 7:** Mariners		**SL:** Best Defensive 3B
1986				**SL:** Best Defensive 3B
1988		**No. 6:** Mariners		
1989		**No. 3:** Mariners		

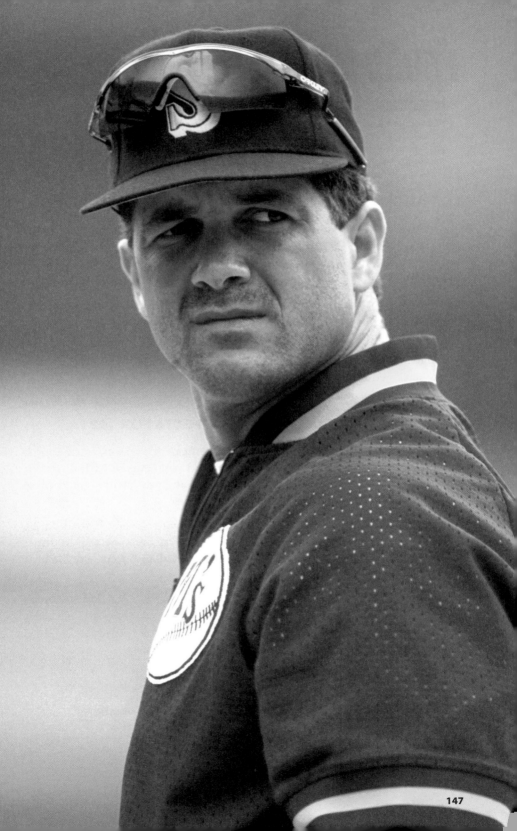

PEDRO MARTINEZ, RHP

BIOGRAPHY

PROPER NAME: Pedro Jaime Martinez.
BORN: October 25, 1971 in Manoguayabo, Dominican Republic.
HT: 5-11. **WT:** 195. **BATS:** R. **THROWS:** R.
FIRST PRO CONTRACT: Signed as international free agent by Dodgers, June 18, 1988.

LOS ANGELES DODGERS TOP 10 PROSPECTS FOR 1991

Martinez has the same lean body as his 6-foot-4, 173-pound brother Ramon, the Dodgers' 20-game winner. Despite being shorter, Pedro concedes nothing to Ramon in his ability to consistently send a 90 mph fastball to the plate. Once he fills out and gets stronger, his velocity will surpass Ramon's.

Martinez has the makings of a good curve and changeup, but both are below-average pitches now. He fields his position well, is a tough and intelligent kid, but often tries to be too fine and goes unnecessarily deep into the count.

Martinez did not play winter ball because of a stress fracture of his right elbow sustained in instructional league.

— Alan Simpson

CALIFORNIA LEAGUE TOP 10 PROSPECTS FOR 1991

Martinez spent just two months in Bakersfield this season, but he made quite an impression. He went 8-0, 2.05 with 83 strikeouts in 61 innings. He was promoted to Double-A San Antonio in May and was pitching for Triple-A Albuquerque by August. Overall, he won 18 games.

The managers selected Martinez as the pitcher with the best fastball. At 20, Martinez is farther along than brother Ramon was at the same age. Martinez has a good changeup and was working on his curveball in Bakersfield. He blew his fastball past hitters in the California League.

— Maureen Delany

MINOR LEAGUE MENTIONS BY BA

YEAR	TOP 100	ORG RANKING	LEAGUE RANKING	BEST TOOLS
1990			No. 3: Pioneer	
1991		No. 8: Dodgers	No. 1: California No. 5: Texas	CAL: Best Pitching Prospect, Best Fastball TL: Best Pitching Prospect
1992	No. 10	No. 1: Dodgers	No. 3: Pacific Coast	PCL: Best Fastball
1993	No. 62	No. 5: Dodgers		

DON MATTINGLY, 1B

BIOGRAPHY

PROPER NAME: Donald Arthur Mattingly. **BORN:** April 20, 1961 in Evansville, Ind.
HT: 6-0. **WT:** 175. **BATS:** L. **THROWS:** L. **SCHOOL:** Reitz Memorial HS, Evansville, Ind.
FIRST PRO CONTRACT: Selected by Yankees in 19th round (493rd overall) of 1979 draft;
signed June 5, 1979.

SOUTHERN LEAGUE TOP 10 PROSPECTS FOR 1981

This lefthander loves to hit and has caught the eye of Yankees owner George Steinbrenner, which never hurts in this organization. Mattingly made the Southern Leauge all-star team as an outfielder, but can handle the glove at first base. His size (6 feet, 175 pounds) and lack of speed are his only drawbacks. He gets a good jump on the ball in left field, although his arm is only average.

Mattingly, only 20 years old, hit .316 for the Western Division champion Sounds. He had 173 hits, including 36 doubles and seven home runs. A contact hitter who sprays the ball with only occasional power, Mattingly impressed Yankees minor league hitting instructor Joe Pepitone.

"Mattingly will only hit for a better average the higher he goes in this game. He'll hit better in the major leagues than he will here," Pepitone said.

The only drawback is finding a position for him. He will probably break in as a designated hitter.

— **Joe Biddle**

INTERNATIONAL LEAGUE TOP 10 PROSPECTS FOR 1982

Mattingly hit nothing but line drives in compiling a .315 average with 10 homers and 75 RBIs. The only question is whether the lefthander will have the power expected of an outfielder/first baseman.

The scouting report: "He has one of the best batting eyes in the league. I don't know how many home runs he'll hit, but he'll get bigger and stronger."

— **Lary Bump**

MINOR LEAGUE MENTIONS BY BA

YEAR	TOP 100	ORG RANKING	LEAGUE RANKING	BEST TOOLS
1981			**No. 4:** Southern	
1982			**No. 6:** International	
1983		**No. 9:** Yankees		

JOE MAUER, C

BIOGRAPHY

PROPER NAME: Joseph Patrick Mauer. **BORN:** April 19, 1983 in St. Paul, Minn. **HT:** 6-5. **WT:** 225. **BATS:** L. **THROWS:** R. **SCHOOL:** Cretin-Derham Hall HS, St. Paul, Minn. **FIRST PRO CONTRACT:** Selected by Twins in first round (first overall) of 2001 draft; signed July 17, 2001.

MIDWEST LEAGUE TOP 10 PROSPECTS FOR 2002

Mark Prior was the consensus top prospect in the 2001 draft, and he needed just seven weeks in the minors before he was ready for the majors. Unable to determine what it would take to sign Prior, who ultimately received a record guarantee of $10.5 million, the Twins chose Mauer. There's absolutely no feeling they wound up with a consolation prize.

Interestingly, managers raved about his skills behind the plate while scouts believed his offense was ahead of his defense. Both camps agreed he only needs time to become an all-around catching star. Mauer should be a .300 hitter capable of 20-30 homers per year. He went deep just four times in 2002, but he's strong and his power will develop as he learns to pull more pitches. His stroke and approach are solid, and he walked more than he struck out.

"He hits like Adam Dunn did when Adam Dunn was in Rockford in 1999," Beloit manager Don Money said. "Adam Dunn didn't pull the ball. He hit the other way, hit the other way, hit the other way like Joe Mauer did. Now look at him."

A Florida State quarterback recruit and high school basketball star, Mauer is extremely athletic for a catcher. He has a strong, accurate arm and quick, effortless release, which allowed him to rank third in the MWL by throwing out 42 percent of basestealers. His biggest needs are learning to call a game and handle a pitching staff.

— **Jim Callis**

MINOR LEAGUE MENTIONS BY BA

YEAR	TOP 100	ORG RANKING	LEAGUE RANKING	BEST TOOLS
2001			**No. 1:** Appalachian	
2002	No. 7	**No. 1:** Twins	**No. 1:** Midwest	**MWL:** Best Defensive C
2003	No. 4	**No. 1:** Twins	**No. 1:** Florida State	**FSL:** Best Hitter, Best Defensive C
2004	No. 1	**No. 1:** Twins	**No. 1:** Eastern	
2005	No. 1	**No. 1:** Twins		

BRIAN McCANN, C

BIOGRAPHY

PROPER NAME: Brian Michael McCann. **BORN:** February 20, 1984 in Athens, Ga.
HT: 6-3. **WT:** 225. **BATS:** L. **THROWS:** R. **SCHOOL:** Duluth (Ga.) HS.
FIRST PRO CONTRACT: Drafted by Braves in second round (64th overall) of 2002 draft;
signed June 11, 2002.

ATLANTA BRAVES TOP 10 PROSPECTS FOR 2004

The son of former Marshall head baseball coach Howard McCann and younger brother of Clemson third base prospect Brad McCann, Brian put together a solid first full season in pro ball. He ranked second in the organization in RBIs and fourth in batting.

Drafted for his offensive potential, McCann has a pretty swing and plenty of raw power. But he's far from one-dimensional, as he's just a tick behind Brayan Pena as the top defensive catcher in the system. McCann's arm strength is good and his accuracy is improving. The Braves also love his hard-nosed attitude behind the plate.

McCann has made strides with his defense, but he's not a sure thing to remain at catcher. He'll need to continue to improve his footwork and agility. He also must stay in shape in order to remain strong throughout the season. He homered just once during the last two months of the season after going deep 11 times in the first three.

He has much more offensive upside than projected 2004 starter Johnny Estrada, and the Braves are thrilled with the progress McCann has shown early in his career. He'll spend 2004 in high Class A.

— **Bill Ballew**

MINOR LEAGUE MENTIONS BY BA

YEAR	TOP 100	ORG RANKING	LEAGUE RANKING	BEST TOOLS
2002			**No. 20:** Gulf Coast	
2003		**No. 28:** Braves	**No. 20:** South Atlantic	
2004		**No. 7:** Braves	**No. 8:** Carolina	**CAR:** Best Defensive C
2005	No. 44	**No. 3:** Braves	**No. 9:** Southern	

ANDREW McCUTCHEN, OF

BIOGRAPHY

PROPER NAME: Andrew Stefan McCutchen. **BORN:** October 10, 1986 in Fort Meade, Fla.
HT: 5-11. **WT:** 195. **BATS:** R. **THROWS:** R. **SCHOOL:** Fort Meade (Fla.) HS.
FIRST PRO CONTRACT: Selected by Pirates in first round (11th overall) of 2005 draft;
signed June 16, 2005.

PITTSBURGH PIRATES TOP 10 PROSPECTS FOR 2006

The Pirates made McCutchen their top pick after he hit .709 as a high school senior. He has good athletic genes; his father played football at Carson-Newman (Tenn.) and his mother played volleyball in junior college in Florida.

McCutchen has a good blend of power and speed, often drawing comparisons to Marquis Grissom. He has wiry strength and his extra-base hit total should increase once his body fills out. He has outstanding speed and a quick first step, enabling him to cover plenty of ground in center field. McCutchen played at a small rural high school and is still somewhat raw in all aspects of the game. His arm is his weakest tool but still grades out as average.

— **John Perrotto**

SOUTH ATLANTIC LEAGUE TOP 10 PROSPECTS FOR 2006

There are few 19-year-olds who make it look as easy as McCutchen, and even fewer who do as many things well.

"He did everything," Lake County manager Lee May Jr. said. "He can cover a lot of ground, steal a base and hit for power. He is a complete ballplayer."

Though he's just 5-foot-10 and 170 pounds and has a very quiet swing, McCutchen is able to generate bat speed and power with his lightning-quick hands. He can drive the ball to all fields and projects as a .300 hitter with above-average pop and speed. McCutchen has well above-average range and looks like a future Gold Glove winner in center field.

— **Matt Meyers**

MINOR LEAGUE MENTIONS BY BA

YEAR	TOP 100	ORG RANKING	LEAGUE RANKING	BEST TOOLS
2005			**No. 1:** Gulf Coast	
2006	No. 50	**No. 2:** Pirates	**No. 1:** South Atlantic	
2007	No. 13	**No. 1:** Pirates	**No. 2:** Eastern	**EL:** Most Exciting Player
2008	No. 13	**No. 1:** Pirates	**No. 2:** International	**IL:** Most Exciting Player
2009	No. 33	**No. 2:** Pirates	**No. 3:** International	**IL:** Fastest Baserunner, Most Exciting Player

BaseBall america

ROCK SOLID

PLUS
Strong Rotation,
Outfield Lead Our
All-Rookie Team

Who's At The Head
Of The Class?
We Send Home
Our Annual
Draft Report Cards

Hometown Hero
Joe Mauer Wins
Major League
Player Of The Year

Comprehensive
Look At Nation's
Top College
Recruiting Classes

Wrap It Up: Our
Holiday Gift Guide

JACK McDOWELL, RHP

BIOGRAPHY

PROPER NAME: Jack Burns McDowell. **BORN:** January 16, 1966 in Van Nuys, Calif.
HT: 6-5. **WT:** 180. **BATS:** R. **THROWS:** R. **SCHOOL:** Stanford.
FIRST PRO CONTRACT: Selected by the White Sox in first round (fifth overall) of 1987 draft;
signed July 29, 1987.

TOP 25 HIGH SCHOOL PROSPECTS FOR 1984 DRAFT

The outstanding prospect in the fertile San Fernando Valley area north of Los Angeles, scouts particularly like McDowell's size (6-5, 180) and makeup (he's already signed with Stanford). Through his first 38 innings this season, McDowell was 5-0 with a 0.37 ERA and had struck out 45 while walking 14. A year ago, he was 7-1 with a 0.85 ERA for Notre Dame.

According to McDowell, his best pitch is his fastball, but he uses a fork-ball for his strikeout pitch. McDowell plays shortstop when not pitching, and through 14 games was hitting .512 with three homers and 19 RBIs.

—Allan Simpson

CHICAGO WHITE SOX TOP 10 PROSPECTS FOR 1988

The fifth player selected last June, McDowell could be the Opening Day starter and is an early favorite for Rookie of the Year.

McDowell was brilliant in four starts for the Sox last September (3-0, 1.93 ERA) after a rough breaking-in period at Sarasota and Birmingham (1-3, 6.51). His problems disappeared after the Sox tightened his delivery, which stabilized his release point.

McDowell's fastball is consistent at 87-89 mph and has been clocked as high as 93 mph. His forkball and slider are power pitches but need to become more consistent. The Sox rave about his maturity and presence on the mound, which is a trait that all pitchers seem to carry out of Stanford.

— Ken Leiker

YEAR	TOP 100	ORG RANKING	LEAGUE RANKING	BEST TOOLS
MINOR LEAGUE MENTIONS BY BA				
1988		**No. 1:** White Sox		

Big League Notebooks, Spring Training Rosters

NL East: Rating the Top 10 Prospects

BaseBall america

"Baseball News You Can't Get Anywhere Else . . ."

March 28, 1988
Price $1.95 ($2.50 in Canada)
Now in Our 8th Year

1988 ROOKIE PREVIEW

White Sox Savior

Jack McDowell: College to Comiskey

Oakland's Walt Weiss: Man in the Middle

Rookie of the Year Again? Is the System Fair?

Caribbean Celebration

Phil Regan Gets a Bath As Escogido Wins It All

Exclusive Coverage And Features

159

FRED McGRIFF, 1B

BIOGRAPHY

PROPER NAME: Frederick Stanley McGriff. **BORN:** October 31, 1963 in Tampa.
HT: 6-3. **WT:** 215. **BATS:** L. **THROWS:** L. **SCHOOL:** Jefferson HS, Tampa.
FIRST PRO CONTRACT: Selected by Yankees in ninth round (233rd overall) of 1981 draft;
signed June 11, 1981.

TORONTO BLUE JAYS TOP 10 PROSPECTS FOR 1985

All right, he still has a ways to go. But once he arrives, McGriff will give people plenty to talk about. Just like Willie Upshaw and Damaso Garcia, who like McGriff were raw talents the Blue Jays stole away from the Yankees' system, McGriff has the ability. It just needs refining.

The only question on when he will make it to the big leagues is when he will make consistent contact. He has struck out 260 times in 894 at-bats the last two minor league seasons, and he probably always will pile up strikeouts. But when he hits the ball, it goes a long way (50 home runs and 136 RBIs the last two years), a tempting sight for the Blue Jays, whose home park is a paradise for lefthanded hitters.

He has made a steady climb in the last two years since the Blue Jays got him as a throw-in in the trade for Dale Murray, having played at Kinston and Florence in 1983 and Knoxville and Syracuse last year.

Like other young power hitters, the curveball throws him for a curve. His defense is still in the marginal category, but he has good lateral movement and an excellent arm. His reactions are slow, but his desire and work habits make him a good learner.

— **Tracy Ringolsby**

MINOR LEAGUE MENTIONS BY BA

YEAR	TOP 100	ORG RANKING	LEAGUE RANKING	BEST TOOLS
1983		**No. 5:** Blue Jays	**No. 5:** Carolina	
1984		**No. 2:** Blue Jays		
1985		**No. 1:** Blue Jays		
1986		**No. 7:** Blue Jays	**No. 4:** International	

MARK McGWIRE, 1B

BIOGRAPHY

PROPER NAME: Mark David McGwire. **BORN:** October 1, 1963 in Pomona, Calif.
HT: 6-5. **WT:** 225. **BATS:** R. **THROWS:** R. **SCHOOL:** Southern California.
FIRST PRO CONTRACT: Selected by the Athletics in the first round (10th overall) of the 1984
draft; signed July 20, 1984.

PACIFIC COAST LEAGUE TOP 10 PROSPECTS FOR 1986

McGwire's totals at Huntsville and Tacoma included a .312 average, 23 homers and 112 RBIs in 133 games before promoted to the A's in August.

"I've never seen a guy with stronger hands and forearms," Tacoma manager Keith Lieppman said. "Even when his weight shift is off, he can use his hands and drive the ball a long way."

McGwire made 41 errors at third base, but only 10 in his final 50 games. He stands 6-foot-5 and was a first baseman when the A's signed him in 1984.

"Once he learns to read the ball off the bat, he'll be OK," Lieppman said. "If guys like Harmon Killebrew and Yogi Berra could play third base, he can too."

— Ken Leiker

OAKLAND ATHLETICS TOP 10 PROSPECTS FOR 1987

The 10th player selected in the 1984 draft, McGwire has the strength in his arms and hands to hit the ball out of the park when he is fooled by a pitch. McGwire is fooled less frequently now that he has tightened his swing and learned to cover the inside of the plate. He progressed faster last season than the A's expected, making superb contact for a man of his size.

McGwire, though, probably isn't ready for the varsity. Even though he bats righthanded, he has some difficulty with lefthanded pitching. And the A's aren't ready to trust him at third base, where he made 47 errors last season.

A first baseman and pitcher at Southern Cal, he was switched to third base after signing with the A's. They remain convinced that he has the agility and reactions to play third, blaming his mistakes on lapses in concentration.

— Ken Leiker

MINER LEAGUE MENTIONS BY BA				
YEAR	**TOP 100**	**ORG RANKING**	**LEAGUE RANKING**	**BEST TOOLS**
1985		No. 5: Athletics	No. 3: California	
1986		No. 6: Athletics	No. 9: Pacific Coast	
1987		No. 3: Athletics		

Will Yankees' Buhner Emerge in 1988?

Look Out, Fenway: Here Comes Sam Horn

Baseball america

"Baseball News You Can't Get Anywhere Else . . ."

July 25-Aug. 9, 1987
Price: $1.95 ($2.50 in Canada)
Now in Our 7th Year

THE 1987 ROOKIE REPORT

Oakland Slugger
Mark McGwire (right);
Montreal's Versatile
Casey Candaele (below)

ALSO INSIDE:

☐ Major League
Columnists

☐ Short Season
Minor Leagues
Statistics Reports

☐ Draft '87
Signings

☐ Amateur
Baseball

☐ And Our
Complete
Coverage
Of All 13
Full-Season
Minor Leagues

College Player of the Year

The Hitting
Machine:
Oklahoma State's
Robin Ventura

■ All-America
Selections

■ Coach of the Year

■ Pitcher of the Year

■ Freshman
All-Americans

YADIER MOLINA, C

BIOGRAPHY

PROPER NAME: Yadier Benjamin Molina. **BORN:** July 13, 1982 in Bayamon, Puerto Rico.
HT: 5-11. **WT:** 205. **BATS:** R. **THROWS:** R. **SCHOOL:** Maestro Ladi HS, Vega Alta, Puerto Rico.
FIRST PRO CONTRACT: Selected by Cardinals in fourth round (113th overall) of 2000 draft;
signed Sept. 6, 2000.

ST. LOUIS CARDINALS TOP 10 PROSPECTS FOR 2003

How loaded was Peoria in 2002? Just three players among the Cardinals' Top 10 didn't play there. Molina, the brother of Angels catchers Benji and Jose Molina, handled a strong pitching staff that led the Midwest League in ERA.

Molina has the catch-and-throw skills to join his brothers in the big leagues. He receives, throws and blocks the ball well, and he handles pitchers well for his age. He threw out 52 percent (49 of 94) of basestealers and turned nine double plays, showing the strength of his arm.

Molina's ceiling depends on his offensive development. The Cardinals are preaching patience and were encouraged by his progress last year. He needs better plate discipline, must keep his strikeouts down and use the whole field.

With defensive skills this good, Molina needs to be merely adequate on offense to be an everyday major league catcher.

— Will Lingo

PACIFIC COAST LEAGUE TOP 10 PROSPECTS FOR 2004

The third Molina brother to catch in the majors—Bengie and Jose are on the Angels—Yadier spent most of the year backing up Mike Matheny in St. Louis. A similar defender with more offensive potential than Matheny, Molina should soon displace him as the starter.

Molina led PCL regulars by throwing out 38 percent of basestealers and was easily the top defensive catcher in the league. His receiving skills are also a plus, though he sometimes has lapses in concentration. He's still developing as a hitter but made strides this year with his plate discipline and bat control.

— Jim Callis

MINOR LEAGUE MENTIONS BY BA

YEAR	TOP 100	ORG RANKING	LEAGUE RANKING	BEST TOOLS
2002		**No. 7:** Cardinals		
2003		**No. 10:** Cardinals		
2004		**No. 4:** Cardinals	**No. 10:** Pacific Coast	**PCL:** Best Defensive C

MIKE MUSSINA, RHP

BIOGRAPHY

PROPER NAME: Michael Cole Mussina. **BORN:** December 8, 1968 in Williamsport, Pa.
HT: 6-2. **WT:** 190. **BATS:** L. **THROWS:** R. **SCHOOL:** Stanford.
FIRST PRO CONTRACT: Selected by Orioles in first round (20th overall) of 1990 draft; signed July 28, 1990.

BALTIMORE ORIOLES TOP 10 PROSPECTS FOR 1991

The Orioles drafted Mussina out of high school in 1987 but couldn't talk him out of a commitment to Stanford. Three years later, Mussina was ready to sign. Working in Double-A and Triple-A last season, he had a 3-0, 1.46 record.

Mussina's next stop might be the Baltimore rotation. He compliments a hard fastball with a curveball and a changeup. Mussina throws a knuckle-curve, but he has trouble controlling it.

Like most Stanford products, he works with poise and intelligence. Some time in Triple-A certainly would be worthwhile, but what Mussina lacks probably could be gained with on-the-job training in the major leagues.

— **Ken Leiker**

INTERNATIONAL LEAGUE TOP 10 PROSPECTS FOR 1991

Mussina, 22, is on the fast track to being an accomplished pitcher in Baltimore. The Orioles' first-round pick out of Stanford University in 1990, he has dominated two leagues in two seasons with a fastball, self-taught knuckle-curve, slider and changeup.

"He's got all the pitches," said one manager. "He throws hard and has good command."

Mussina finished second in the IL in ERA (2.87), behind Richmond's Armando Reynoso (2.61).

— **Tim Pearrell**

MINOR LEAGUE MENTIONS BY BA

YEAR	TOP 100	ORG RANKING	LEAGUE RANKING	BEST TOOLS
1990			No. 9: Eastern	
1991	No. 19	No. 2: Orioles	No. 3: International	IL: Best Pitching Prospect, Best Breaking Pitch

DAVID ORTIZ, DH

BIOGRAPHY

PROPER NAME: David Americo Ortiz. **BORN:** November 18, 1975 in Santo Domingo, D.R.
HT: 6-3. **WT:** 230. **BATS:** L. **THROWS:** L. **SCHOOL:** Estudia Espillat, Dominican Republic.
FIRST PRO CONTRACT: Signed as international free agent by Mariners, Nov. 28, 1992.

EASTERN LEAGUE TOP 10 PROSPECTS FOR 1997

Size and power always bring comparisons. Ortiz, acquired from the Mariners and formerly known as David Arias, has both size and power, and now he's starting to draw the comparisons. Willie McCovey, Dave Parker and a pre-injury Cliff Floyd. Not bad company.

"He fits in that category," [Binghamton manager Rick] Sweet said. "He shows tremendous power. He doesn't swing at a lot of bad pitches. He needs to work on his defense, but as an offensive player, he's one of the best in the league."

— **Andrew Linker**

MINNESOTA TWINS TOP 10 PROSPECTS FOR 1998

BACKGROUND: Signed by the Mariners when he went by the last name Arias, Ortiz was acquired by the Twins in September 1996 to complete a deal for Dave Hollins. He was Minnesota's minor league player of the year after starting the year in Class A and finishing in the big leagues.

STRENGTHS: Ortiz is a lefthanded power hitter who should flourish in the Metrodome. He has driven in 223 runs in the last two minor league seasons.

WEAKNESSES: Ortiz will catch what he gets to, but to avoid being a DH he needs to work on his movement. At the plate, he could also be more selective.

FUTURE: The Twins' signing of Orlando Merced should remove the temptation to push Ortiz too fast. He can open the 1998 season at Triple-A Salt Lake.

— **Tracy Ringolsby**

MINOR LEAGUE MENTIONS BY BA

YEAR	TOP 100	ORG RANKING	LEAGUE RANKING	BEST TOOLS
1996			**No. 6:** Midwest	**MWL:** Best Defensive 1B, Most Exciting Player
1997			**No. 6:** Eastern	
1998		**No. 2:** Twins		

ROY OSWALT, RHP

BIOGRAPHY

PROPER NAME: Roy Edward Oswalt. **BORN:** August 29, 1977 in Kosciusko, Miss.
HT: 6-0. **WT:** 190. **BATS:** R. **THROWS:** R. **SCHOOL:** Holmes (Miss.) JC.
FIRST PRO CONTRACT: Selected by Astros in 23rd round (684th overall) of 1996 draft;
signed May 18, 1997.

HOUSTON ASTROS TOP 10 PROSPECTS FOR 2001

BACKGROUND: One way the Astros try to keep player-development costs down is by using the draft-and-follow process. They identify raw players and try to sign them after they refine their skills in junior college. Their best work may have been done with Oswalt, though he didn't come cheap. He blossomed so much that he would have been a first-round pick had Houston not handed him a $500,000 bonus as a 23rd-round pick in 1996.

STRENGTHS: Oswalt pitched under control in 2000, which is why his career took off. He still pitches up in the strike zone at times, but for the most part he worried about painting the black at 92-94 mph rather than trying to reach back and throw 96. Righthanders have absolutely no chance when he throws his heat knee-high on the outside corner. He hides the ball well, and when he doesn't try to max out his velocity, his fastball explodes out of his hand with late life. Oswalt's curveball jumps straight down, and his changeup at times is a third above-average pitch. He's stingy with walks and home runs and limited lefthanders to a .201 average in Double-A.

WEAKNESSES: Oswalt needs to remember that less is more when it comes to his fastball and that he has more command and movement when he throws in the low 90s. He needs more consistency with his curveball and changeup, which he doesn't always finish off.

FUTURE: If he continues to progress like he did last year, Oswalt will be ready for Houston after a half-season in Triple-A. He has the stuff to be a No. 1 starter down the road.

— Jim Callis

MINOR LEAGUE MENTIONS BY BA

YEAR	TOP 100	ORG RANKING	LEAGUE RANKING	BEST TOOLS
1999		**No. 9:** Astros		
2000			**No. 3:** Florida State **No. 1:** Texas	**TL:** Best Control
2001	No. 13	**No. 1:** Astros		

JAKE PEAVY, RHP

BIOGRAPHY

PROPER NAME: Jacob Edward Peavy. **BORN:** May 31, 1981 in Mobile, Ala.
HT: 6-1. **WT:** 195. **BATS:** R. **THROWS:** R. **SCHOOL:** St. Paul's Episcopal HS, Mobile, Ala.
FIRST PRO CONTRACT: Selected by Padres in 15th round (472nd overall) of 1999 draft;
signed June 9, 1999.

ARIZONA LEAGUE TOP 10 PROSPECTS FOR 1999

Peavy was only a 15th-round draft choice, but to Arizona League hitters he pitched like a premium pick. He won the league's pitching triple crown. Peavy throws his fastball 87-91 mph with plus movement and complements it with a hard curveball and a straight change.

"He just dominated everyone," AZL Athletics manager John Kuehl said.

— **David Rawnsley**

SAN DIEGO PADRES TOP 10 PROSPECTS FOR 2001

The Padres spent four first-round picks on pitchers in 1999, but 15th-rounder Peavy has their best pitcher from that draft so far. He lasted that long because he was considered frail, wild and committed to an Auburn scholarship.

Peavy used a fastball that reaches the mid-90s, good slider and nice change-up to tie for the Class A Midwest League lead in strikeouts last season. He makes it tougher for hitters by varying his arm angle and pitching down in the strike zone. His control has been better than expected as a pro. He has allowed just 10 homers in 208 innings and hasn't had any trouble with lefthanders.

To this point, he hasn't shown a significant weakness. Like all young pitchers, he can refine his command and the consistency of his pitches. Peavy's pure stuff isn't as good as that of Wascar Serrano, Gerik Baxter and Mark Phillips. It's his pitching savvy that elevates him ahead of them on this list, and it will be interesting to see if it can keep him there. Peavy will move up to high Class A Lake Elsinore in 2001 and could reach Double-A late in the season.

— **Jim Callis**

MINOR LEAGUE MENTIONS BY BA

YEAR	TOP 100	ORG RANKING	LEAGUE RANKING	BEST TOOLS
1999			**No. 7:** Arizona	
2000			**No. 7:** Midwest	**MWL:** Best Pitching Prospect
2001	No. 40	**No. 2:** Padres	**No. 5:** California	
2002	No. 28	**No. 3:** Padres	**No. 1:** Southern	

DUSTIN PEDROIA, 2B

BIOGRAPHY

PROPER NAME: Dustin Luis Pedroia. **BORN:** August 17, 1983 in Woodland, Calif.
HT: 5-9. **WT:** 175. **BATS:** R. **THROWS:** R. **SCHOOL:** Arizona State.
FIRST PRO CONTRACT: Selected by Red Sox in second round (65th overall) of 2004 draft;
signed July 21, 2004.

BOSTON RED SOX TOP 10 PROSPECTS FOR 2007

Since he was Boston's top pick (second round) in 2004, Pedroia consistently has hit .300 and stayed at shortstop in spite of scouts' belief he'll have to eventually move to second base. He continually draws David Eckstein comparisons, though he has more pop and less speed than the World Series MVP does.

Pedroia has some of the best hand-eye coordination in baseball. That allows him to make consistent contact while swinging from his heels, which in turn gives him gap power. He led the Triple-A International League by averaging just one strikeout per 18.3 plate appearances, and he fanned just seven times in 89 big league at-bats.

His instincts make him an effective defender and baserunner. Surehanded, he has made just 17 errors in 301 pro games. Pedroia is undersized and needs to get stronger so he can avoid the nagging injuries (wrist and shoulder) that have bothered him the last two years. His speed, range and arm strength are all below-average, but that hasn't stopped him yet.

The Red Sox signed free agent Julio Lugo to start at shortstop, but they also let Mark Loretta depart, leaving an opening at second base. That's the best fit for Pedroia, the frontrunner to claim the starting job there.

— **Jim Callis**

MINOR LEAGUE MENTIONS BY BA

YEAR	TOP 100	ORG RANKING	LEAGUE RANKING	BEST TOOLS
2005		**No. 6:** Red Sox	**No. 12:** Eastern **No. 17:** International	**EL:** Best Strike-Zone Judgment, Best Defensive 2B
2006	No. 77	**No. 5:** Red Sox	**No. 18:** International	
2007		**No. 7:** Red Sox		

ANDY PETTITTE, LHP

BIOGRAPHY

PROPER NAME: Andrew Eugene Pettitte. **BORN:** June 15, 1972 in Baton Rouge, La.
HT: 6-5. **WT:** 225. **BATS:** L. **THROWS:** L. **SCHOOL:** San Jacinto (Texas) JC.
FIRST PRO CONTRACT: Selected by Yankees in 22nd round (594th overall) of 1990 draft;
signed May 25, 1991.

NEW YORK YANKEES ORG. REPORT, FEB. 1995

Andy Pettitte remembers well a talk he had with pitching coach Nardi Contreras after he was pounded in his first two starts at Triple-A Columbus last summer.

"Right now, you're terrible," Contreras told the lefthander. "You were a good Double-A pitcher, but Double-A is not Triple-A."

Pettitte, 22, responded to the challenge so well that the Yankees named him their 1994 minor league pitcher of the year. Shortstop Derek Jeter, named Baseball America's Minor League Player of the Year, was an obvious choice as player of the year.

Pettitte gives Contreras much of the credit, not only for his candor but also for his instruction.

"He got me throwing my pitches a lot sharper and turned me around," Pettitte said. "He taught me how to set up hitters, and you have to do that in Triple-A because they are a lot smarter hitters."

Contreras persuaded Pettitte, a 22nd-round pick in 1990 who signed with the Yankees the next spring as a draft-and-follow, to abandon his slow curveball in favor of a harder breaking ball.

"Every day we'd be out there spinning curveballs," Pettitte said. "The slow curve gave them more time to react. They could sit on it. With the break a lot harder down, I was able to get more ground balls."

When Pettitte attended instructional league, Yankees pitching coach Billy Connors taught him a cut fastball, and he is using the offseason to work on that.

— **Tom Pedulla**

MINOR LEAGUE MENTIONS BY BA

YEAR	TOP 100	ORG RANKING	LEAGUE RANKING	BEST TOOLS
1994		**No. 7:** Yankees		
1995	No. 49	**No. 3:** Yankees		

MIKE PIAZZA, C

BIOGRAPHY

PROPER NAME: Michael Joseph Piazza. **BORN:** September 14, 1968 in Norristown, Pa.
HT: 6-3. **WT:** 215. **BATS:** R. **THROWS:** R. **SCHOOL:** Miami-Dade JC.
FIRST PRO CONTRACT: Selected by Dodgers in 62nd round (1,390th overall) of 1988 draft;
signed July 11, 1988.

LOS ANGELES DODGERS TOP 10 PROSPECTS FOR 1992

Piazza is [Tommy] Lasorda's godson and was drafted in the 62nd round as a favor, with nobody giving him even a remote chance to make it. But the kid is big, strong and devoted, and all he does is bomb home runs everywhere he plays, including the Mexican Pacific League this winter.

Expectations are higher now, as is the Double-A competition. As a catcher, his arm is improving, but he still has much to learn about receiving. Nonetheless, his power and ability to make contact are making people take notice.

After two mediocre seasons in short-season ball and the Florida State League, Piazza began showing something with the bat at high Class-A Bakersfield in 1991, when he hit 29 homers and had an OPS of .884. After a tremendous 1992 season at Double-A San Antonio and Triple-A Albuquerque, he went to the Arizona Fall League and impressed.

— **Ken Gurnick**

PACIFIC COAST LEAGUE TOP 10 PROSPECTS FOR 1992

Nevermind Piazza's much-publicized ties. This kid has the tools to be a front-line big league catcher.

The godson of Tommy Lasorda started the season in Double-A, but finished with the Dodgers and went 3-for-3 in his big league debut. Power is his best asset. He doesn't pull the ball much, which concerns some, but he can reach the deepest fences in the yard, so what does it matter?

He has an above-average arm, though he could use a little more consistency. Piazza greatly improved his receiving skills this year.

— **Mike Klis**

MINOR LEAGUE MENTIONS BY BA

YEAR	TOP 100	ORG RANKING	LEAGUE RANKING	BEST TOOLS
1991				**CAL:** Best Power
1992		**No. 10:** Dodgers	**No. 5:** Pacific Coast	
1993	No. 38	**No. 1:** Dodgers		

179

JORGE POSADA, C

BIOGRAPHY

PROPER NAME: Jorge Rafael Posada. **BORN:** August 17, 1971 in Santurce, Puerto Rico.
HT: 6-2. **WT:** 215. **BATS:** B. **THROWS:** R. **SCHOOL:** Calhoun (Ala.) JC.
FIRST PRO CONTRACT: Selected by Yankees in 24th round (646th overall) of 1990 draft; signed May 24, 1991.

NEW YORK YANKEES TOP 10 PROSPECTS FOR 1997

BACKGROUND: Posada enjoyed his best minor league season in 1996, earning International League all-star honors. His uncle, former big leaguer Leo Posada, is a minor league hitting instructor for the Dodgers. His father Jorge scouts Puerto Rico for the Rockies.

STRENGTHS: A converted shortstop, Posada features quick hands and a quick release. He lacks Mike Figga's pure arm strength but is a more accomplished all-around receiver.

WEAKNESSES: Posada has no obvious weaknesses. His power and overall hitting skill continue to evolve.

FUTURE: After three years in Triple-A, Posada is ready for the big time. He'll serve in a backup role with the Yankees in 1997 and should be a starter down the road, with a ceiling of a .270-.280 average and 20 homers a season.

— **Allan Simpson**

MINOR LEAGUE MENTIONS BY BA

YEAR	TOP 100	ORG RANKING	LEAGUE RANKING	BEST TOOLS
1995		**No. 7:** Yankees		
1997		**No. 10:** Yankees		

DAVID SEELIG/ALLSPORT | ISSUE DATE: SEPTEMBER, 2007

BASEBALL AMERICA

Double Trouble

Switch-hitters like Yankees star Jorge Posada are producing numbers that give pitchers nightmares

Special Section: Your First Look At Hottest New Equipment Ideas

Showcases, All-Star Games Kick Off Scouting For 2008 Draft

Our Columnists Weigh In On Baseball's Latest Milestones

Complete Lineup Of Prospect Profiles: Daric Barton, Jair Jurrens, Hainley Statia, Hector Gomez, Ben Revere

BUSTER POSEY, C

BIOGRAPHY

PROPER NAME: Gerald Dempsey Posey. **BORN:** March 27, 1987 in Leesburg, Ga.
HT: 6-1. **WT:** 210. **BATS:** R. **THROWS:** R. **SCHOOL:** Florida State.
FIRST PRO CONTRACT: Selected by Giants in first round (fifth overall) of 2008 draft;
signed Aug. 15, 2008.

CALIFORNIA LEAGUE TOP 10 PROSPECTS FOR 2009

Now that Matt Wieters has graduated to the major leagues, Posey is the top catching prospect in baseball. Hitting .326/.416/.531 and throwing out 49 percent of basestealers at San Jose bolstered his reputation, and he earned promotions to Triple-A Fresno and later to San Francisco.

Posey is a strong and athletic catcher with no obvious flaw in his game. He's a mature hitter with strength, a good setup and the ability to use the entire field. He runs very well for a catcher and has a slightly above-average arm.

The only question with Posey is how well he'll handle the premium stuff of Tim Lincecum and Matt Cain in San Francisco.

— **Dave Perkin**

PACIFIC COAST LEAGUE TOP 10 PROSPECTS FOR 2010

Posey blistered PCL pitching during his time in the league and has no glaring flaws as a hitter. He has a balanced swing and keeps his bat in the hitting zone for a long time with excellent plate coverage. He controls the strike zone and drives balls to all fields, rarely getting fooled. His power is still developing, but he projects to be an annual 20-homer threat.

"I put him down as the best hitter in the league," Salt Lake manager Bobby Mitchell said. "He's far advanced for his age, as a hitter especially, and he's proven it. He's gone up to the big leagues and done a great job for them."

Posey famously struggled with handling quality stuff early in his pro career, but he has come a long way defensively. He improved his set-up behind the plate, as well as his footwork on his throws. He used his strong arm to erase 44 percent of PCL basestealers, and he also garnered praise for his leadership.

— **Jim Shonerd**

MINOR LEAGUE MENTIONS BY BA

YEAR	TOP 100	ORG RANKING	LEAGUE RANKING	BEST TOOLS
2009	No. 14	**No. 2:** Giants	**No. 1:** California **No. 1:** Pacific Coast	**CAL:** Best Defensive C
2010	No. 7	**No. 1:** Giants	**No. 1:** Pacific Coast	**PCL:** Best Hitter

DAVID PRICE, LHP

BIOGRAPHY

PROPER NAME: David Taylor Price. **BORN:** August 26, 1985 in Murfreesboro, Tenn.
HT: 6-5. **WT:** 215. **BATS:** L. **THROWS:** L. **SCHOOL:** Vanderbilt.
FIRST PRO CONTRACT: Selected by Devil Rays in first round (first overall) of 2007 draft;
signed Aug. 15, 2007.

TAMPA BAY RAYS TOP 10 PROSPECTS FOR 2009

Few players have lived up to the hype, both before and after being the No. 1 overall pick in the draft, better than Price.

Price rates off the charts with his stuff, athleticism and disposition, a package that should make him one of the premier pitchers in the majors. He has two plus-plus pitches with a mid-90s fastball and a biting slider. His fastball has outstanding movement with late arm-side run. His slider is reminiscent of John Smoltz's with its depth and 87-88 mph velocity. He blew away the Red Sox with both pitches in the ALCS clincher, generating several awkward swings. His changeup also can be an above-average offering with impressive deception and fade. Price has the ability to add and subtract velocity from his pitches, and he uses the entire strike zone to his advantage. He receives as much praise for his makeup and humility as he does for his pitching, which is saying a lot. He was unfazed when asked to pitch in pressure situations in the playoffs.

Price lacks full confidence in his changeup. He didn't need that third pitch in college and the minors, but he must trust it more and improve its depth to succeed as a big league ace. He never has encountered failure, so he has yet to show he can make the necessary adjustments when the inevitable occurs, but he should be up to the challenge.

Extremely goal-oriented, Price wants to join the Rays' rotation to open the 2009 season. He has the talent and work ethic to make that happen. Even if he falls short, it won't be long before he's part of Tampa Bay's rotation for good, and he eventually should become the No. 1 starter on the talented staff.

It would be no surprise if he moved to the forefront of the game's elite pitchers at a pace similar to that of Tim Lincecum.

— **Bill Ballew**

MINOR LEAGUE MENTIONS BY BA

YEAR	TOP 100	ORG RANKING	LEAGUE RANKING	BEST TOOLS
2008	No. 10	**No. 2:** Rays	**No. 2:** Southern	**SL:** Best Pitching Prospect
2009	No. 2	**No. 1:** Rays		

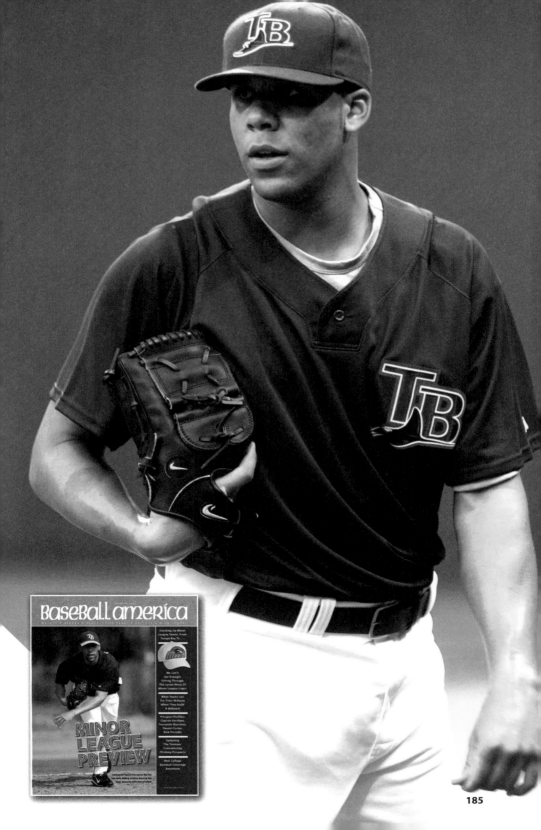

KIRBY PUCKETT, OF

BIOGRAPHY

PROPER NAME: Kirby Puckett. **BORN:** March 14, 1960 in Chicago.
HT: 5-8. **WT:** 210. **BATS:** R. **THROWS:** R. **SCHOOL:** Triton (Ill.) JC
FIRST PRO CONTRACT: Selected by Twins in first round (third overall) of 1982 January draft.

MINNESOTA TWINS TOP 10 PROSPECTS FOR 1984

The Twins' first-round selection in the January 1982 draft, Puckett is built along the lines of former big league outfielder Jim Wynn and shows promises of producing along the same lines as Wynn, too.

He broke in with a flurry at Elizabethon, earning MVP honors in the Appalachain League in 1982, when he hit .362 and stole 43 bases. And he kept on knocking them over at Visalia last year, when he produced with the bat (.314, 29 doubles, seven triples, nine home runs and 97 RBIs), with his feet (48 stolen bases) and his glove.

He has outstanding speed and uses it both offensively and defensively. He has a strong arm, and he can also hit. More than that, he has great instincts, both on the bases and in the field. He also adapts well to new ideas.

He can come in a hurry if the Twins are so inclined. And once he does make it to the big leagues, he promises to be a crowd favorite. Not only does he have ability, but he has charisma.

"He's got a bubbly personality," one California League observer said. "He's the kind of kid that walks on the field and the fans fall in love with him. The way he goes about playing the game creates an enthusiasm that is transmitted to the people in the stands."

— **Tracy Ringolsby**

MINOR LEAGUE MENTIONS BY BA

YEAR	TOP 100	ORG RANKING	LEAGUE RANKING	BEST TOOLS
1982			**No. 7:** Appalachian	
1983		**No. 4:** Twins	**No. 5:** California	**CAL:** Best Outfield Arm
1984		**No. 1:** Twins		

ALBERT PUJOLS, 1B

BIOGRAPHY

PROPER NAME: Jose Alberto Pujols. **BORN:** January 16, 1980 in Santo Domingo, Dominican Republic. **HT:** 6-3. **WT:** 240. **BATS:** R. **THROWS:** R. **SCHOOL:** Maple Woods (Mo.) JC. **FIRST PRO CONTRACT:** Selected by Cardinals in 13th round (402nd overall) of 1999 draft; signed Aug. 17, 1999.

ST. LOUIS CARDINALS TOP 10 PROSPECTS FOR 2001

The Cardinals offered Pujols $10,000 to sign in 1999, so he went to the summer amateur Jayhawk League instead and hit .343 with five home runs and 17 RBIs, good enough to earn a bonus close to $60,000. Then he proved to be a bargain, with a monster pro debut in which he was the MVP of the Class A Midwest League and the Pacific Coast League playoffs. He followed up by hitting .323 in the Arizona Fall League.

Pujols started hitting in instructional league just after he signed and hasn't stopped. He uses the whole field and has great strike-zone discipline. He goes the other way well and should add power as he moves up. He's still young, but he has the approach of a veteran. He has a strong arm at third base.

Pujols wasn't a more notable amateur prospect because he was much heavier and didn't move well. He's in good shape now, but the Cardinals aren't sure about his defense. He's passable at third, but he already has played a few games in the outfield and could wind up there.

Pujols must have been sad to see 2000 end. The Cardinals are trying to temper expectations after just one pro season, but he could be in the big leagues by 2002, especially with the void at third base created by the Fernando Tatis trade. He likely will start 2001 at Double-A New Haven.

— **Will Lingo**

MINOR LEAGUE MENTIONS BY BA

YEAR	TOP 100	ORG RANKING	LEAGUE RANKING	BEST TOOLS
2000				**MWL:** Best Hitter, Best Defensive 3B, Best INF Arm
2001	No. 42	**No. 2:** Cardinals		

MANNY RAMIREZ, OF

BIOGRAPHY

PROPER NAME: Manny Aristides Ramirez. **BORN:** May 30, 1972 in Santo Domingo, Dominican Republic. **HT:** 6-0. **WT:** 225. **BATS:** R. **THROWS:** R. **SCHOOL:** Washington HS, New York. **FIRST PRO CONTRACT:** Selected by Indians in first round (13th overall) of 1991 draft; signed June 5, 1991.

1993
MiLB PLAYER OF THE YEAR

CLEVELAND INDIANS TOP 10 PROSPECTS FOR 1992

It's been a long time since any first-year Indians player hit with the impact that Ramirez did in nearly winning the Appalachian League triple crown. Voted the MVP and top prospect in the league, Ramirez exceeded even the most optimistic hopes.

Ramirez had little trouble adjusting to wooden bats. His .679 slugging percentage led all of professional baseball.

"He did some things as an 18-year-old that some guys in the big leagues can't do," said Johnny Goryl, Indians director of minor league field operations.

Drafted as a third baseman/outfielder, Ramirez showed enough defensively to get slotted as a center fielder. The kid just needs to play. And the Indians need to guard against rushing him.

— Jim Ingraham

CAROLINA LEAGUE TOP 10 PROSPECTS FOR 1992

Every manager wondered what kind of numbers Ramirez would have posted if he hadn't been injured. The Indians' first-round pick in 1991 struggled early in the season, baffled by the breaking pitches in the Carolina League.

But the 20-year-old made adjustments and was tearing up the league before a bruised hand, suffered while swinging, ended his season in early July.

"Before he got hurt, he was probably the best player in this league," Frederick manager Bobby Miscik said. "He's got all the tools."

— Dean Gyorgy

MINOR LEAGUE MENTIONS BY BA

YEAR	TOP 100	ORG RANKING	LEAGUE RANKING	BEST TOOLS
1991			**No. 1:** Appalachian	
1992	No. 37	**No. 3:** Indians	**No. 3:** Carolina	**CAR:** Most Exciting Player
1993	No. 13	**No. 1:** Indians	**No. 2:** Eastern	**EL:** Best Hitter
1994	No. 7	**No. 1:** Indians		

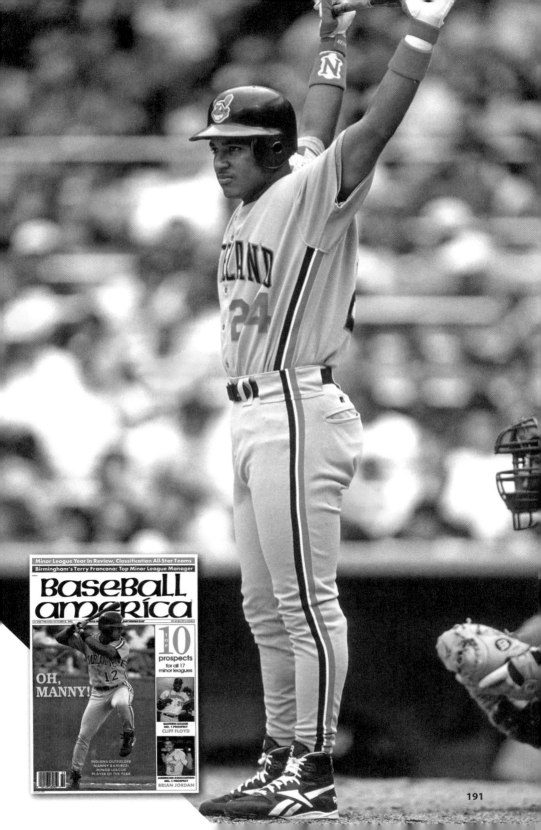

MARIANO RIVERA, RHP

BIOGRAPHY

PROPER NAME: Mariano Rivera. **BORN:** November 29, 1969 in Panama City, Panama.
HT: 6-2. **WT:** 195. **BATS:** R. **THROWS:** R. **SCHOOL:** La Chorrea, Panama City, Panama.
FIRST PRO CONTRACT: Signed as international free agent by Yankees, Feb. 17, 1990.

NEW YORK YANKEES TOP 10 PROSPECTS FOR 1993

Rivera's three-year career has been slowed by injury. He missed the first third of the 1992 season nursing a stiff elbow, made 10 starts, then went down for good and succumbed to elbow surgery. Still, he was placed on the Yankees' 40-man roster.

When healthy, Rivera gives the Yankees plenty to contemplate. He broke into pro ball with a sterling 0.17 ERA in the GCL and pitched one memorable inning late in the 1992-93 Venezuelan winter season, striking out big leaguers Gus Polidor, Luis Salazar and Andres Galarraga on 10 pitches.

Rivera has increased his velocity on his fastball from 87 mph to 94 mph since signing, and he has excellent command of three pitches. He's scheduled to pitch in Double-A in 1993, elbow permitting.

— **Allan Simpson**

MINOR LEAGUE MENTIONS BY BA

YEAR	TOP 100	ORG RANKING	LEAGUE RANKING	BEST TOOLS
1993		**No. 9:** Yankees		
1995		**No. 9:** Yankees		

ALEX RODRIGUEZ, SS

BIOGRAPHY

PROPER NAME: Alexander Enmanuel Rodriguez. **BORN:** July 27, 1975 in New York.
HT: 6-3. **WT:** 230. **BATS:** R. **THROWS:** R. **SCHOOL:** Westminster Christian HS, Miami.
FIRST PRO CONTRACT: Selected by Mariners in first round (first overall) of 1993 draft;
signed Aug. 30, 1993.

MIDWEST LEAGUE TOP 10 PROSPECTS FOR 1994

Rodriguez dazzled more with his hitting than his fielding, but he has exceptional major league talent in both areas. Midwest League managers rated his arm, power and speed above-average big league tools.

"Alex has a good swing and a lot of range," Appleton manager Carlos Lezcano said. "But I think the best thing about Alex is that he is eager to learn the game. He applies what you teach him very quickly.

"Alex is a take-charge kind of guy. I think it was good for him to get a taste of the big leagues this year. I think he's going to stay up there all year next year and for a long time to come."

— Curt Rallo

PACIFIC COAST LEAGUE TOP 10 PROSPECTS FOR 1995

Rodriguez, the No. 1 overall pick in 1993, already was noted for batting skills and defensive prowess despite his large frame. This season, his mental approach was put to the test. Rodriguez was yo-yoed from Seattle to Tacoma three times, but he persevered.

In one stretch, he hit home runs in six of seven games, many of them mammoth, 400-foot-plus shots. Tacoma manager Steve Smith noted Rodriguez for his positive influence in the clubhouse. He always talked about the team first.

"Rodriguez' approach is admirable," Salt Lake manager Phil Roof said. "The only negative, and it might not even be one, is his size. If he gets bigger, he might have to move to third base, but he can excel there just as much."

— Javier Morales

MINOR LEAGUE MENTIONS BY BA

YEAR	TOP 100	ORG RANKING	LEAGUE RANKING	BEST TOOLS
1994	No. 6	**No. 1:** Mariners	**No. 1:** Midwest	**MWL:** Best Hitter, Best Defensive SS, Best INF Arm, Most Exciting Player
1995	No. 1	**No. 1:** Mariners	**No. 1:** Pacific Coast	**PCL:** Best INF Arm, Most Exciting Player

FRANCISCO RODRIGUEZ, RHP

BIOGRAPHY

PROPER NAME: Francisco Jose Rodriguez. **BORN:** January 7, 1982 in Caracas, Venezuela.
HT: 6-0. **WT:** 195. **BATS:** R. **THROWS:** R. **SCHOOL:** Juan Lovera, Caracas, Venezuela.
FIRST PRO CONTRACT: Signed as international free agent by Angels, Sept. 24, 1998.

PIONEER LEAGUE TOP 10 PROSPECTS FOR 1999

The diminutive Rodriguez was the Angels' first big bonus venture into Latin America when he signed last winter. Rodriguez already throws 94-95 mph with excellent life and tops out at 97 mph.

"He was throwing 95-96 with a slider from hell," Medicine Hat manager Paul Elliot said. "It was like a man against boys, except he's just a boy himself."

There was some concern among managers that Rodriguez throws too much across his body. In addition to his fastball, Rodriguez throws a slider, curveball and changeup, with the slider being his top secondary pitch.

— **David Rawnsley**

TEXAS LEAGUE TOP 10 PROSPECTS FOR 2002

The live-armed Rodriguez had been touted in the Angels' organization since he signed for a $900,000 bonus in 1998. Because of injuries and inconsistent performance, though, the results never measured up to the promise.

Moved to the bullpen, Rodriguez took off. He jumped to Triple-A and then to Anaheim in September, where he pitched well in the playoff race. Rodriguez was a different pitcher in relief, bringing two plus pitches to the mound. His fastball was 93-96 mph, and his slider is already a major league out-pitch.

"He should be a great setup guy and grow into the role of closer, like Mariano Rivera," Arkansas manager Doug Sisson said. "He has the aptitude, competitiveness, makeup and stuff."

— **Will Lingo**

MINOR LEAGUE MENTIONS BY BA

YEAR	TOP 100	ORG RANKING	LEAGUE RANKING	BEST TOOLS
1999			**No. 1:** Pioneer	
2000		**No. 2:** Angels		
2001	No. 71	**No. 2:** Angels		
2002		**No. 7:** Angels	**No. 5:** Texas **No. 12:** Pacific Coast	
2003	No. 10	**No. 1:** Angels		

IVAN RODRIGUEZ, C

BIOGRAPHY

PROPER NAME: Ivan Rodriguez. **BORN:** November 30, 1971 in Vega Baja, Puerto Rico.
HT: 5-9. **WT:** 205. **BATS:** R. **THROWS:** R. **SCHOOL:** Lino Padron Rivera, Vega Baja, Puerto Rico.
FIRST PRO CONTRACT: Signed as international free agent by Rangers, July 27, 1988.

TEXAS RANGERS TOP 10 PROSPECTS FOR 1991

Pudge Rodríguez will play the entire 1991 season as a 19-year-old and already has scouts saying he could hold his own in the big leagues. He's a two-time all-star in the minor leagues and was selected as the No. 1 prospect in the Florida State League by the managers.

Defensively, he is at the head of the class, and offensively he has produced at a higher level than the Rangers hoped for in both years. He is only 5-foot-10 but has a solid body that makes him appear bigger. His small stature gives him good mobility behind the plate, where he blocks balls on a big league standard.

There's no question about his arm. Luis Rosa, a scout now with the Chicago Cubs, rates him as a cross between Benito Santiago and Sandy Alomar Jr., two All-Star catchers signed by Rosa. He is consistently timed between 1.7 to 1.75 seconds getting the ball to second base, rivaling the arm strength of Santiago. But he does it with mechanics more along the lines of Alomar. There's no toss from the knees or sidearm deliveries.

Despite his youth, Rodríguez shows take-charge ability behind the plate. The Rangers feel they have good young pitching, but Rodríguez is the one who has to handle them and in two years his staffs have finished first and second in their league in ERA. And yes, he is allowed to call his own game.

— **Tracy Ringolsby**

MINOR LEAGUE MENTIONS BY BA

YEAR	TOP 100	ORG RANKING	LEAGUE RANKING	BEST TOOLS
1989			**No. 7:** South Atlantic	
1990			**No. 1:** Florida State	**FSL:** Best Defensive C
1991	No. 7	**No. 1:** Rangers	**No. 1:** Texas	**TL:** Best Defensive C

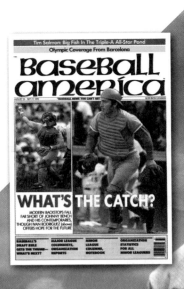

SCOTT ROLEN, 3B

BIOGRAPHY

PROPER NAME: Scott Bruce Rolen. **BORN:** April 4, 1975 in Jasper, Ind.
HT: 6-4. **WT:** 245. **BATS:** R. **THROWS:** R. **SCHOOL:** Jasper (Ind.) HS.
FIRST PRO CONTRACT: Selected by Phillies in second round (46th overall) of 1993 draft;
signed July 22, 1993.

SOUTH ATLANTIC LEAGUE TOP 10 PROSPECTS FOR 1994

Rolen plays third base with passion, range and arm strength. He has excellent hand-eye coordination and foot speed, as one would expect of an athlete offered a basketball scholarship to the University of Georgia.

Rolen also impressed managers with his ability to hit for both power and average.

"He's one of the best third baseman I've ever seen in a long time." Hickory manager Fred Kendall said. "He's a tough kid and he knows what he's doing at the plate."

— **Gene Sapakoff**

FLORIDA STATE LEAGUE TOP 10 PROSPECTS FOR 1995

Rolen played just 66 FSL games before getting promoted to Double-A Reading. He made a can't-miss impression with his skills and attitude.

He showed good gap power and has a strong arm. He needs to work on minimizing the size of his strike zone and improving his defensive consistency.

"He's going to play for the Phillies for a long time," Daytona manager Dave Trembley said. "He's got a good, strong body. He'll hit a lot of doubles and home runs, and he's going to be something on turf. He also plays a lot older than he is."

— **Sean Kernan**

MINOR LEAGUE MENTIONS BY BA

YEAR	TOP 100	ORG RANKING	LEAGUE RANKING	BEST TOOLS
1994			**No. 9:** South Atlantic	**SAL:** Best Defensive 3B
1995	No. 91	**No. 1:** Phillies	**No. 1:** Florida State	
1996	No. 27	**No. 1:** Phillies	**No. 2:** Eastern	**EL:** Best Defensive 3B
1997	No. 13	**No. 1:** Phillies		

BaseBall america

MAJORS • MINORS • PROSPECTS • DRAFT • COLLEGE • HIGH SCHOOL

Special Section:
Our Fall
Equipment
Guide

Team USA
Takes Gold In
World
University
Championship

West Gets
Revenge In
Second Annual
AFLAC Classic

From the majors on down,
the game experiences
record-setting
popularity this summer

BASEBALL'S
BIGGEST YEAR

Early Look At
Draft Class Of
2005: Scouting
Reports On Top
College, High
School Players

JIMMY ROLLINS, SS

BIOGRAPHY

PROPER NAME: James Calvin Rollins. **BORN:** November 27, 1978 in Oakland, Calif.
HT: 5-7. **WT:** 175. **BATS:** B. **THROWS:** R. **SCHOOL:** Encinal HS, Alameda, Calif.
FIRST PRO CONTRACT: Selected by Phillies in second round (46th overall) of 1996 draft;
signed June 24, 1996.

PHILADELPHIA PHILLIES TOP 10 PROSPECTS FOR 2000

BACKGROUND: The Phillies soured on Rollins after a mediocre 1998 season and a perceived lackadaisical attitude. A new staff saw a different player in 1999. Rollins improved his skills on the field and became a leader on both teams he played for.

STRENGTHS: Though only 5-foot-8, Rollins plays with the skills of a bigger player. He is smooth and quick in the infield with a plus arm from the hole and no fear around the bag. Rollins is equally proficient from both sides of the plate and has surprising pop for his size. He stays under control at the plate and doesn't overswing.

WEAKNESSES: As long as Rollins maintains a solid approach, continues to polish his skills on routine plays and learns the nuances of baserunning and situational hitting, he has a bright big league future. He has all the tools.

FUTURE: The Phillies' middle infield is wide open. Rollins was playing well in the Venezuelan League, and it wouldn't be a shock if Rollins made his big league debut next summer.

— **David Rawnsley**

MINOR LEAGUE MENTIONS BY BA

YEAR	TOP 100	ORG RANKING	LEAGUE RANKING	BEST TOOLS
1997			**No. 10:** South Atlantic	
1998		**No. 4:** Phillies		
1999		**No. 11:** Phillies		
2000	No. 95	**No. 4:** Phillies		
2001	No. 31	**No. 1:** Phillies		

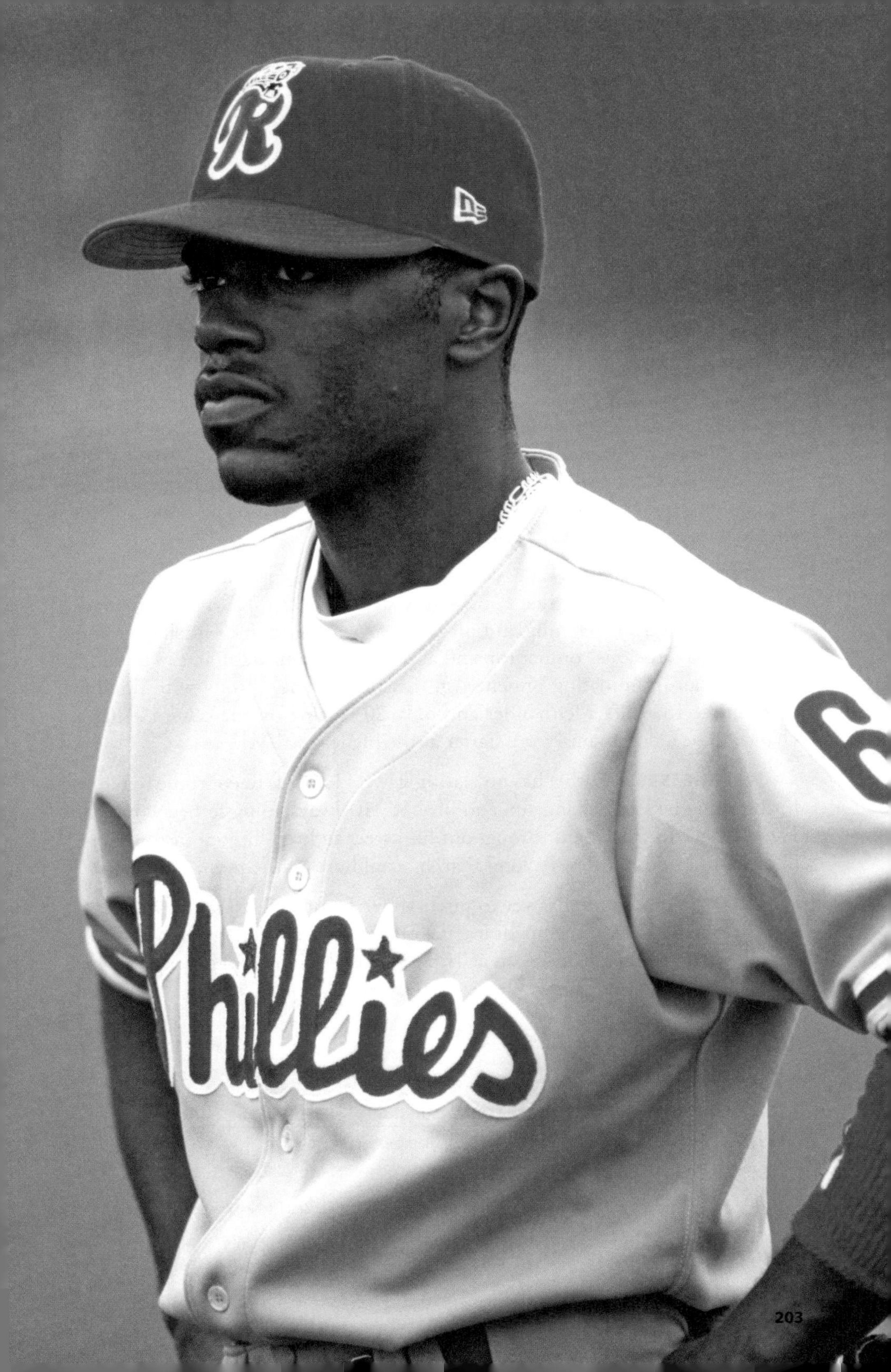
Phillies

C.C. SABATHIA, LHP

BIOGRAPHY

PROPER NAME: Carsten Charles Sabathia. **BORN:** July 21, 1980 in Vallejo, Calif.
HT: 6-6. **WT:** 300. **BATS:** L. **THROWS:** L. **SCHOOL:** Vallejo (Calif.) HS.
FIRST PRO CONTRACT: Selected by Indians in first round (20th overall) of 1998 draft;
signed by June 28, 1998.

CLEVELAND INDIANS TOP 10 PROSPECTS FOR 2001

BACKGROUND: It would be difficult for any player to have a wider range of experience than Sabathia had during the 2000 season. In addition to pitching in high Class A and Double-A, Sabathia also was selected to the Eastern League all-star team, participated in the Futures Game, pitched in the Hall of Fame game at Cooperstown and finished the season with the big league club in September, though he never was formally activated. Sabathia also was among the finalists for the U.S. Olympic team.

STRENGTHS: Sabathia is the whole package—and a gigantic one at that. He has a tremendous fastball that consistently sits at 97-98 mph, a good change-up, a terrific feel for pitching and off-the-charts makeup. He's intelligent and coachable, a ferocious competitor, and at 6-foot-7 and upward of 260 pounds, he can be an intimidating presence on the mound. He's strong with durable mechanics. That he's a lefthander and only 20 is icing on the cake. He has a chance to be a dominant No. 1 starter at the big league level.

WEAKNESSES: Sabathia has no glaring flaws. He needs to continue to refine his breaking ball and changeup, and his body is always going to be a concern. He will have to work hard throughout his career to keep himself in top shape in order to avoid injuries. Beyond that, he could use a little more experience.

FUTURE: Though he has yet to pitch above Double-A, Sabathia will get a chance to win a spot in the major league rotation in the spring. Sabathia would benefit from at least a half-season at Triple-A Buffalo, but team officials are going to let his talent dictate where he starts 2001.

— Jim Ingraham

MINOR LEAGUE MENTIONS BY BA

YEAR	TOP 100	ORG RANKING	LEAGUE RANKING	BEST TOOLS
1998			**No. 3:** Appalachian	
1999		**No. 2:** Indians		
2000	No. 57	**No. 1:** Indians	**No. 1:** Carolina **No. 2:** Eastern	**EL:** Best Pitching Prospect, Best Fastball
2001	No. 7	**No. 1:** Indians		

Looking Back At The Minor Leagues, 25 And 50 Years Ago

Baseball America

Big lefthander
C.C. Sabathia
hurls toward Cleveland

AL
TOP 10
PROSPECTS

Is Tom Kelly The Right Man For The Twins?

Complete 40-Man Rosters

Full Winter Ball Report

BRET SABERHAGEN, RHP

BIOGRAPHY

PROPER NAME: Bret William Saberhagen. **BORN:** April 11, 1964 in Chicago Heights, Ill.
HT: 6-1. **WT:** 195. **BATS:** R. **THROWS:** R. **SCHOOL:** Grover Cleveland HS, Reseda, Calif.
FIRST PRO CONTRACT: Selected by Royals in 19th round (480th overall) of 1982 draft;
signed July 26, 1982.

KANSAS CITY ROYALS TOP 10 PROSPECTS FOR 1984

A meteoric rise? No, it's been quicker than that. Mainly a shortstop in high school, Saberhagen's pitching days were limited his senior year in high school because of a tendonitis problem.

He did, however, make a few trips to the mound, and the Royals figured he was worthy of a 19th-round selection in the 1982 draft. It took a while to get Saberhagen, who had a full ride to Southern California, to agree to terms, so he didn't make his pro debut until last summer. It was worth waiting for.

His biggest tool is control. While splitting the season between Ft. Myers of the Florida State League and Jacksonville of the Southern League (where he was a combined 16-7), Saberhagen gave up on 164 hits and 48 walks in 187 innings. And for an encore, he walked only two batters in 47 innings of work in the Instructional League.

He's got a slightly better than average fastball, sometimes getting up to 89 mph with excellent movement. More than that, he keeps the ball near the knees. He also has an outstanding changeup. He still needs to be more consistent with a breaking pitch—he throws both a slider and a curveball.

And Saberhagen also has control of his emotions.

"It's not very often a kid comes along with his kind of maturity," one scout said. "He not only has the physical ability, but he already has emotional maturity.

— **Tracy Ringolsby**

MINOR LEAGUE MENTIONS BY BA

YEAR	TOP 100	ORG RANKING	LEAGUE RANKING	BEST TOOLS
1983			No. 5: Florida State	
1984		No. 2: Royals		

Moonlighting: A Look At Players' Offseason Pursuits

Baseball Down Under: America's Pastime Catches On In Australia

BASEBALL
america

METS· AMORPHOSIS

TOP 10
PROSPECTS
NL EAST

MONTREAL
SHORTSTOP
WILFREDO
CORDERO
TOPS IN A DEEP
EXPOS CROP

NEW EXPOS REGIME
PLANS A CHANGE IN PHILOSOPHY

WHERE COLLEGE BASEBALL IS KING:
AUSTIN, FRESNO, HONOLULU, MIAMI

THE INCREASED FOCUS
ON VISION STUDIES

A PLAYER'S PERSPECTIVE
ON WINTER BASEBALL

MAJOR LEAGUE
ORGANIZATION REPORTS

CHRIS SALE, LHP

BIOGRAPHY

PROPER NAME: Christopher Allen Sale. **BORN:** March 30, 1989 in Lakeland, Fla.
HT: 6-6. **WT:** 180. **BATS:** L. **THROWS:** L. **SCHOOL:** Florida Gulf Coast.
FIRST PRO CONTRACT: Selected by White Sox in first round (13th overall) of 2010 draft;
signed June 20, 2010.

CHICAGO WHITE SOX TOP 10 PROSPECTS FOR 2011

Sale not only became the first player from the 2010 draft to reach the big leagues, he also finished the season closing games for a contender. The White Sox signed Sale for the slot recommendation of $1.656 million—along with the promise that he'd get every opportunity to race through the minors. He made his big league debut on Aug. 6, faster than any draftee since the Reds' Ryan Wagner in 2003.

Sale has the stuff and lanky build to be a facsimile of future Hall of Famer Randy Johnson, throwing three plus pitches from a low three-quarter delivery. His fastball ranged from 90-95 mph with outstanding late life when he worked as a starter in college, and he averaged 96 mph out of the bullpen in the majors. He hit 100 mph three times in a game against the Royals.

Chicago considered his changeup his best pitch when it drafted him—GM Ken Williams compares it to Mark Buehrle's—but he didn't use it much out of the bullpen. Sale used his slider more as a reliever, and it also played up, sitting in the high 80s and topping out at 90 mph. That was important as his slider was questioned coming into the draft. His command is solid, though his arm angle leads to times when he doesn't stay on top of his pitches and leaves them up in the zone.

Sale is unusually poised, capable of making adjustments and pitching out of trouble. Some scouts wonder how durable Sale will be because of his skinny frame, arm action and low slot. He has no history of arm problems, however. Despite his immediate bullpen impact, the White Sox plan to develop Sale as a starter. If he stays healthy, he has the stuff to be a frontline starter or a closer.

— **Phil Rogers**

MINOR LEAGUE MENTIONS BY BA

YEAR	TOP 100	ORG RANKING	LEAGUE RANKING	BEST TOOLS
2011	No. 20	**No. 1:** White Sox		

JOHAN SANTANA, LHP

BIOGRAPHY

PROPER NAME: Johan Alexander Santana. **BORN:** March 13, 1979 in Tovar, Venezuela.
HT: 6-0. **WT:** 210. **BATS:** L. **THROWS:** L. **SCHOOL:** Liceo Jose Nucete Sardi, Venezuela.
FIRST PRO CONTRACT: Signed as international free agent by Astros, July 2, 1995.

MINNESOTA TWINS TOP 10 PROSPECTS FOR 2000

BACKGROUND: The Twins, with the first pick, acquired Santana in a pre-arranged Rule 5 trade with the Marlins in December. He must make the Twins' Opening Day roster or be offered back to the Astros, his former organization. It might be a longshot for him to stick because he has no experience above the Midwest League.

STRENGTHS: Santana has a loose, live arm and a fastball that ranges anywhere from 88-94 mph. He throws a good curveball with a wide, sweeping break and an advanced changeup for his age. Santana's command of the strike zone and his success in winter ball in Venezuela improve his chances of sticking in Minnesota.

WEAKNESSES: The history of the Rule 5 draft is littered with pitchers who couldn't make the jump from low Class A to the big leagues, or whose careers were harmed by the attempt. Santana must handle the big league environment and the possible inactivity.

FUTURE: Unless Santana fails in spring training, the Twins have committed themselves to carrying him as the third reliever in the bullpen behind Eddie Guardado and Travis Miller.

— **David Rawnsley**

MINOR LEAGUE MENTIONS BY BA

YEAR	TOP 100	ORG RANKING	LEAGUE RANKING	BEST TOOLS
2000		No. 8: Twins		

BaseBall america

MAJORS • MINORS • PROSPECTS • DRAFT • COLLEGE • HIGH SCHOOL

Twins ace Johan Santana's approach and stuff have made him the most dominant pitcher in the game and our Major League Player of the Year

THE SURE THING

Holiday Gift Guide: What The Fan In Your Life Will Be Looking For Under The Tree

Who's At The Head Of The Class As We Hand Out Draft Report Cards?

At Long Last, Matt Harrington Comes To Organized Baseball

Billy Beane Assesses Oakland's Season

MAX SCHERZER, RHP

BIOGRAPHY

PROPER NAME: Maxwell M. Scherzer. **BORN:** July 27, 1984 in St. Louis.
HT: 6-3. **WT:** 215. **BATS:** R. **THROWS:** R. **SCHOOL:** Missouri.
FIRST PRO CONTRACT: Selected by D-backs in first round (11th overall) of 2006 draft;
signed May 31, 2007.

SOUTHERN LEAGUE TOP 20 PROSPECTS FOR 2007

Just before Scherzer would have re-entered the 2006 draft, the D-backs coughed up a four-year major league contract worth $4.3 million in guaranteed money to sign the 11th overall pick from 2005. Nicknamed "Max-a-million" by his teammates, he made three starts in high Class A before arriving to Double-A Mobile in late June.

Scherzer's most attractive attribute is a sinking fastball that tops out near 95 mph. His mechanics need some work, as his release point is inconsistent and there's some effort to his delivery, but he does achieve good extension out front and his arm strength is obvious. Scherzer has a two-seamer he can run up to 90 mph, an 80-84 mph slider and a changeup, all of which have potential to be solid-average to plus offerings.

But Scherzer's arsenal is inconsistent, and his overall command is below-average. That leads some scouts to project he'll wind up in the bullpen, where he can focus on his fastball and slider.

"It's an outstanding arm who needs polish and has some max effort to it, which impacts his ability to command the baseball," one scout said. "The stuff is there, it's just a matter of if he can make that next step and command it."

— **Alan Matthews**

MINOR LEAGUE MENTIONS BY BA

YEAR	TOP 100	ORG RANKING	LEAGUE RANKING	BEST TOOLS
2007			No. 15: Southern	
2008	No. 66	No. 4: D-backs	No. 3: Pacific Coast	

CURT SCHILLING, RHP

BIOGRAPHY

PROPER NAME: Curtis Montague Schilling. **BORN:** November 14, 1966 in Anchorage.
HT: 6-5. **WT:** 235. **BATS:** R. **THROWS:** R. **SCHOOL:** Yavapai (Ariz.) JC.
FIRST PRO CONTRACT: Selected by Red Sox in secound round (39th overall) of 1986 January draft; signed May 30, 1986.

SCHILLING READY, WILLING, ABLE TO LEARN

ROCHESTER, N.Y. — The measure of Curt Schilling's season may have been a 3-2 changeup he threw against the Richmond Braves.

"It was the first time in my life," Schilling, a Rochester righthander, said. "Even up 'til this year, I've always been a power pitcher. I have to mix it up in the count, and I have the confidence to do it.

"Guys get called up and you think, 'Maybe I'm next,'" said Schilling, acquired by the Orioles last season from Boston in the Mike Boddicker trade. "I pretty much feel they planned all the way to leave me here all year. … My focus now is to learn and do everything I can for next year."

If the 3-2 changeup is any indication, Schilling has been a model pupil.

"When we started together this spring, I told him I wanted him to establish some goals," pitching coach Dick Bosman said. "One of the biggest goals was I wanted him to get 200 innings. I knew if you could achieve that goal, a lot of things would take care of themselves."

Schilling pitched 119 innings in 17 starts, and recorded decisions in 15. The 200 innings seems within reach, though Schilling came down with a sore shoulder after his start against Richmond.

— **Patti Singer**

BALTIMORE ORIOLES TOP 10 PROSPECTS FOR 1990

Another strong youngster on the verge, Schilling almost was called up five times last year but didn't arrive until September after 13 wins at Rochester.

The delays seemed to affect him as his efficiency trailed off in the second half, but he has the arm, the stuff and the build to be a winner in the majors. He needs only to settle down.

— **Kent Baker**

MINOR LEAGUE MENTIONS BY BA

YEAR	TOP 100	ORG RANKING	LEAGUE RANKING	BEST TOOLS
1990		**No. 2:** Orioles		

Baseball america

Garrido Helps Texas Hook Its Fifth College World Series Title

MIDSEASON UPDATE

HEADHEAD

GARY SHEFFIELD, OF

BIOGRAPHY

PROPER NAME: Gary Antonian Sheffield. **BORN:** November 18, 1968 in Tampa.
HT: 6-0. **WT:** 215. **BATS:** R. **THROWS:** R. **SCHOOL:** Hillsborough HS, Tampa.
FIRST PRO CONTRACT: Selected by Brewers in first round (sixth overall) of 1986 draft;
signed June 26, 1986.

CALIFORNIA LEAGUE TOP 10 PROSPECTS FOR 1987

Sheffield was selected lower than second on only one ballot after driving in a league-leading 103 runs. A second-half slump dropped his average to .277.

"He will be an impact player on the major league level," said Fresno's R.J. Harrison. "A change to the outfield will hasten his progress."

Even the manager who picked Sheffield low, Visalia's Dan Schmitz, was effusive in his praise. "Strong body," Schmitz said. "He can run, field, throw, hit, hit for power, he's an RBI man … has all the tools. He'll be a star."

— Jim Alexander

MILWAUKEE BREWERS TOP 10 PROSPECTS FOR 1989

At 19, he bolted through Double-A and Triple-A last season, leading the minors in RBIs (119) and total bases (294), ranking second in home runs (28) and runs (112) and fifth in hits (116).

Sheffield once was described by the late Harvey Kuenn as a young Willie Mays. He has no apparent weaknesses at the plate because he adjusts on breaking pitches so well, and his power is growing into league-leading proportions. Honing his once-blocky build has helped him remain an above-average runner.

Sheffield has become proficient at shortstop and third base, and his arm plays way above sufficient at both positions. Left field also could be an immediate possibility, if it's where he fits best into the lineup.

— Ken Leiker

MINOR LEAGUE MENTIONS BY BA

YEAR	TOP 100	ORG RANKING	LEAGUE RANKING	BEST TOOLS
1986			**No. 1:** Pioneer	
1987		**No. 1:** Brewers	**No. 1:** California	**CAL:** Best Hitter, Best INF Arm
1988		**No. 1:** Brewers	**No. 2:** Texas **No. 2:** American Association	**TL:** Best Hitter, Best Power
1989		**No. 1:** Brewers		

How Nashville Runs Two Minor League Teams In One City

Home Run Trot: High School Player Of The Year Trot Nixon

BASEBALL america

MARLINS MANIA!

NEWCOMER
GARY SHEFFIELD
FUELS FLORIDA'S
BASEBALL FEVER

BUILDING THE IMPERFECT BEAST

PHILLIES, TIGERS
EXCEED EXPECTATIONS
WITH UNUSUAL
BLUEPRINTS
FOR SUCCESS

MAJOR LEAGUE, MINOR LEAGUE MIDSEASON UPDATES

JOHN SMOLTZ, RHP

BIOGRAPHY

PROPER NAME: John Andrew Smoltz. **BORN:** May 15, 1967 in Warren, Mich.
HT: 6-3. **WT:** 220. **BATS:** R. **THROWS:** R. **SCHOOL:** Waverly HS, Lansing, Mich.
FIRST PRO CONTRACT: Selected by Tigers in 22nd round (574th overall) of 1985 draft;
signed Sept. 22, 1985.

DETROIT TIGERS TOP 10 PROSPECTS FOR 1987

The Tigers took a shot in the dark by drafting Smoltz in the 22nd round of the 1985 draft, then came up with what it took at the 11th hour to convince him to sign instead of playing baseball at Michigan State.

Signing late cost him his 1985 season, and an elbow injury put a damper on 1986. He was 4-0 with a 1.57 ERA at Class A Lakeland before being hurt. Initially, he came back and was tentative in throwing the ball, but by the end of the season was going strong again.

He needs to smooth out his mechanics, but he has a legitimate fastball, good, straight changeup and both a hard and soft curveball.

— **Tracy Ringolsby**

EASTERN LEAGUE TOP 10 PROSPECTS FOR 1987

Whenever you hear Smoltz' name, you hear "great arm" mentioned quickly afterward. The Tigers traded Smoltz to Atlanta late in the season for Doyle Alexander.

Smoltz has a blazing fastball, but he didn't have the control of it to get Double-A hitters out consistently and had a relatively high ERA.

"He'll blow you away for an inning or two and show way above-average stuff," Reading manager George Culver said. "He'll look like a big league pitcher. But then he will lose it and show nothing special. That's why I think you'll see him as a relief pitcher."

— **Kevin Iole**

MINOR LEAGUE MENTIONS BY BA

YEAR	TOP 100	ORG RANKING	LEAGUE RANKING	BEST TOOLS
1986		**No. 9:** Tigers	**No. 5:** Florida State	
1987		**No. 2:** Tigers	**No. 9:** Eastern	**EL:** Best Fastball
1988		**No. 6:** Braves	**No. 1:** International	**IL:** Best Pitching Prospect, Best Fastball, Best Breaking Pitch
1989		**No. 4:** Braves		

BLAKE SNELL, LHP

BIOGRAPHY

PROPER NAME: Blake Ashton Snell. **BORN:** December 4, 1992 in Seattle.
HT: 6-4. **WT:** 215. **BATS:** L. **THROWS:** L. **SCHOOL:** Shorewood HS, Shoreline,
Wash. **FIRST PRO CONTRACT:** Selected by Rays in supplemental first round
(52nd overall) of 2011 draft; signed June 16, 2011.

2015 MiLB PLAYER OF THE YEAR

SOUTHERN LEAGUE TOP 10 PROSPECTS FOR 2015

Snell began the season as a wild but tantalizing lefthander with no high-minors experience, but he ended the campaign as the Minor League Player of the Year after ranking as the SL's finest pitching prospect and reaching Triple-A Durham in late July.

He didn't allow a run in his first eight appearances of the season as he marched to a minor league ERA title with an overall mark of 1.41 that only Justin Verlander (1.29 in 2005) has surpassed in the past 23 seasons.

Snell throws a plus fastball that sits at 93 mph and can bump 96 mph. That velocity and life allows him to work up in the zone when warranted. His plus changeup is so effective that he can double- and triple-up on the pitch to get back into counts or put batters away.

Just as encouragingly, Snell sharpened his breaking ball and incorporated a cutter in 2015, both in an effort to attack the legion of righthanders he will see from here on out. All of his pitches come out of the same arm slot and look to the batter like his fastball.

Snell's athleticism and controlled delivery allowed him to throw more strikes this season—he walked 3.6 batters per nine innings at three levels—than he had since Rookie-ball in 2012. He profiles as a strong No. 2 starter, with the only criticism being that he leans more on raw stuff than pitchability.

— **Matt Eddy**

MINOR LEAGUE MENTIONS BY BA

YEAR	TOP 100	ORG RANKING	LEAGUE RANKING	BEST TOOLS
2011			**No. 13:** Gulf Coast	
2012		**No. 20:** Rays	**No. 4:** Appalachian	
2013		**No. 9:** Rays		
2014		**No. 14:** Rays		
2015		**No. 9:** Rays	**No. 5:** Southern	**FSL:** Best Changeup **SL:** Best Pitching Prospect, Best Changeup
2016	No. 12	**No. 1:** Rays	**No. 6:** International	

BaseBall America

FINAL MINOR
LEAGUE
STATISTICS

MINOR LEAGUE &
ASSOCIATION
ALL-STAR TEAMS

A.J. REED
NEARLY PULLS
COLLEGE-MINORS
POY DOUBLE

LEFTY BLAKE SNELL BECOMES THE
FOURTH RAYS FARMHAND TO WIN
BA'S MINOR LEAGUE AWARD

**PLAYER OF
THE YEAR**

SAMMY SOSA, OF

BIOGRAPHY

PROPER NAME: Samuel Peralta Sosa.
BORN: November 12, 1968 in San Pedro de Macoris, Dominican Republic.
HT: 6-0. **WT:** 225. **BATS:** R. **THROWS:** R. **SCHOOL:** San Pedro de Macoris, Dominican Republic.
FIRST PRO CONTRACT: Signed as international free agent by Rangers, July 30, 1985.

GULF COAST LEAGUE TOP 10 PROSPECTS FOR 1986

A 17-year-old from San Pedro de Macoris in the Dominican Republic, Sosa nearly became a member of the Philadelphia Phillies organization. A Phillies scout, since fired, recognized his talent early and signed him at age 15 with the intent of hiding him until he became legal to sign at age 17. But the scout was fired first, and the Rangers jumped into the void.

Sosa hit just .207 over his first 30 games in the GCL, but then hit .321 the rest of the way to raise his average to .275. He led the league with 19 doubles.

"He has a short swing and the ball just jumps off his bat," said Royals manager Luis Silverio.

— Danny Knobler

TEXAS RANGERS TOP 10 PROSPECTS FOR 1988

It's a coin flip in deciding who belongs No. 1 and who winds up No. 2 between Sosa and fellow outfielder Juan Gonzalez.

Sosa, signed as a free agent out of the Dominican in 1986, won't have the big power numbers of Gonzalez, but he will drive the ball and will be a step ahead in speed. He stole 22 bases last year but hasn't yet scratched the surface.

In the last year, the dramatic improvement has come with Sosa's defense. Sosa was charged with six errors in the Florida Instructional League, where he was voted the Rangers' MVP. Only one came on a dropped fly ball, when he raced into right center field and attempted to backhand a ball in his first game. The other five came on throws, but he also had 11 assists in 32 games.

— Tracy Ringolsby

YEAR	TOP 100	ORG RANKING	LEAGUE RANKING	BEST TOOLS
1986			**No. 4:** Gulf Coast	
1987	**No. 2:** Rangers			
1988	**No. 2:** Rangers			
1989	**No. 2:** Rangers	**No. 9:** Texas		
1990	**No. 2:** White Sox			

Opening Day Rosters For Every Major And Minor League Team

BaseBall america

Did you see that?

Sammy Sosa and Mark McGwire enjoy a midsummer Cubs-Cardinals game at Wrigley Field, one of the must-see events that every true fan needs to experience

College Midseason Update

Complete Minor League Coverage

The Biggest Surprises On Opening Day Rosters

GIANCARLO STANTON, OF

BIOGRAPHY

PROPER NAME: Giancarlo Cruz-Michael Stanton. **BORN:** November 8, 1989 in Panorama, Calif.
HT: 6-6. **WT:** 245. **BATS:** R. **THROWS:** R. **SCHOOL:** Notre Dame HS, Sherman Oaks, Calif.
FIRST PRO CONTRACT: Selected by Marlins in second round (76th overall) of 2007 draft;
signed Aug. 11, 2007.

FLORIDA STATE LEAGUE TOP 10 PROSPECTS FOR 2009

Managers loved to talk about Stanton's power, which allows him to hit the ball out to all parts of the park. They discussed his physicality and ability to make adjustments, but more than anything they talked about his work ethic.

Many noted Stanton's willingness to improve and put in his work on humid Florida afternoons. He showed the eagerness to learn of a struggling utility infielder despite having the ability to get by on his sheer talent. Stanton doesn't have to cheat to hit for power, instead staying back and trusting his hands.

He'll always strike out frequently because his long arms and power-oriented swing creates holes, but he makes adjustments well. He has plus speed, above-average range for an outfielder and a strong arm.

— **J.J. Cooper**

SOUTHERN LEAGUE TOP 10 PROSPECTS FOR 2010

Stanton finished second in the SL in home runs—despite playing just 53 Double-A games before the Marlins called him up on June 6. But pop never has been an issue for Stanton, who has 80 power on the 20-80 scale.

He refined his approach even more in 2010, chasing fewer pitches out of the zone. Stanton still strikes out about once a game, but scouts say that's more a function of his long arms and swing than his strike-zone awareness.

Not only are his hands well-positioned and his stroke full of leverage, but Stanton has learned to study pitchers' plans of attack. Stanton also made big strides with his reads, jumps and throwing accuracy in right field. His speed and arm strength are average, and he's an aggressive defender with plus range.

— **Ian Gordon**

MINOR LEAGUE MENTIONS BY BA

YEAR	TOP 100	ORG RANKING	LEAGUE RANKING	BEST TOOLS
2008		**No. 11:** Marlins	**No. 3:** South Atlantic	**SAL:** Best Power
2009	No. 16	**No. 2:** Marlins	**No. 1:** Florida State **No. 4:** Southern	**FSL:** Best Power **SAL:** Best Power
2010	No. 3	**No. 1:** Marlins	**No. 1:** Southern	**SL:** Best Hitter, Best Power

MARLINS
Baseball America
MIDSEASON PROSPECT REPORT
flying fish
Checking In On Every Organization: Whose Stock Is Up, Who Needs To Turn It Around?
Minor League All-Star Team, Plus Surprise And Rookie Squads
Roundup Of International Signings, With Inside Look At Dominican Recruiting Process
South Atlantic League Mourns Death Of Moss

STEPHEN STRASBURG, RHP

BIOGRAPHY

PROPER NAME: Stephen James Strasburg. **BORN:** July 20, 1988 in San Diego.
HT: 6-5. **WT:** 235. **BATS:** R. **THROWS:** R. **SCHOOL:** San Diego State.
FIRST PRO CONTRACT: Selected by Nationals in first round (first overall) of 2009 draft;
signed Aug. 17, 2009.

WASHINGTON NATIONALS TOP 10 PROSPECTS FOR 2010

Strasburg went undrafted out of high school in 2006 because of questions about his conditioning, work ethic and maturity. Three years later, he was the No. 1 pick and regarded by many scouts as the best prospect in draft history.

Strasburg is a once-in-a-generation talent. His plus-plus fastball sits in the mid- to upper 90s, and the Nationals have seen him hit 102 mph. His breaking ball rates as a second plus-plus offering, a power, 81-84 mph curveball that he can throw for strikes or use as a chase pitch. Even when he doesn't stay on top of it, it's a tough pitch, becoming more of a hard slider. He also flashes a plus changeup, though he seldom needed the pitch to dominate in college. Strasburg has excellent control with all of his pitches, and he also has very advanced command within the strike zone. He's athletic, physical and durable, and he earns raves for his makeup both on and off the field.

The only thing Strasburg doesn't have is pro experience. The general consensus is that there are no red flags in his delivery, as his arm action is fairly loose and he uses his legs well. But it should be noted that there are some within the organization who are concerned that he eventually could break down because he locks out his elbow on his follow through, putting torque on his shoulder.

Strasburg figures to compete for a job in the major league rotation in spring training, and he might never throw a pitch in the minors, though Washington might also choose to ease him into pro ball with an assignment to Double-A or Triple-A. He projects as a true No. 1 starter and a Cy Young Award winner, and anything less will be a disappointment.

— **Aaron Fitt**

MINOR LEAGUE MENTIONS BY BA

YEAR	TOP 100	ORG RANKING	LEAGUE RANKING	BEST TOOLS
2010	No. 2	**No. 1:** Nationals		

DARRYL STRAWBERRY, OF

BIOGRAPHY

PROPER NAME: Darryl Eugene Strawberry. **BORN:** March 12, 1962 in Los Angeles.
HT: 6-6. **WT:** 200. **BATS:** L. **THROWS:** L. **SCHOOL:** Crenshaw HS, Los Angeles.
FIRST PRO CONTRACT: Selected by Mets in first round (first overall) of 1980 draft;
signed July 11, 1980.

TEXAS LEAGUE TOP 10 PROSPECTS FOR 1982

Baseball's No. 1 draft pick by the Mets in 1980, he was voted the Texas League's Most Valuable Player in 1981, and deservedly so. While hitting .283, but spending most of the season hovering around the .300 mark, Strawberry led the league in home runs with 34 and bases on balls with 100. His 97 RBIs ranked third, and his 45 stolen bases tied him for second.

At 6-foot-5 and with base-stealing speed, Strawberry can cover the ground in right field. He also has a strong arm, albeit a tad undisciplined. His power is amazing, as he hit some of the longest home runs seen in the league, and he learned in the latter half of the season to take the outside pitch to left field.

The Mets brass keep saying he will be brought along slowly, but the wait is getting shorter. Called up to Triple-A for the International League playoffs in September, he was instrumental in leading Tidewater to the Governor's Cup.

— **Mickey Spagnola**

NEW YORK METS TOP 10 PROSPECTS FOR 1983

He began to feel more comfortable with his role as a future star in New York last summer after batting just .255 with Lynchburg (Carolina) in 1981.

"His skills could allow him to be something awfully special if he continues to develop them," one Mets scout said.

Strawberry can run, hit with power, has good arm strength and is fast developing into a solid defensive player. There is an outside chance that he could open 1983 in right field for the Mets.

— **Ron Morris**

MINOR LEAGUE MENTIONS BY BA				
YEAR	**TOP 100**	**ORG RANKING**	**LEAGUE RANKING**	**BEST TOOLS**
1981			**No. 3:** Carolina	
1982			**No. 1:** Texas	
1983		**No. 1:** Mets		

ICHIRO SUZUKI, OF

BIOGRAPHY

PROPER NAME: Ichiro Suzuki. **BORN:** October 22, 1973 in Kasugai, Japan.
HT: 5-11. **WT:** 175. **BATS:** L. **THROWS:** R. **SCHOOL:** Aikoudai Meiden, Nagoya, Japan.
FIRST PRO CONTRACT: Selected by Orix in fourth round of 1992 Japanese draft; signed by Mariners, Nov. 30, 2000.

SEATTLE MARINERS TOP 10 PROSPECTS FOR 2001

Known by the single-name moniker of Ichiro in his homeland, he is the seven-time defending batting champion in Japan's Pacific League. He attended spring training with the Mariners in 1999, and when the Orix Blue Wave made him available to major league teams, Seattle bid $13.125 million for the right to sign him, then inked him to a three-year, $22 million deal.

Ichiro has been compared to Wade Boggs and Tony Gwynn as a hitter because he rarely strikes out and uses the entire field. Some scouts believe he'll contend for the American League batting crown right away. He runs well and has the speed and ability to play center field or either of the corners. He owns an accurate arm that plays well, even in right field.

The biggest knock on him has been a lack of power, but like Boggs and Gwynn, he may have the ability to hit for more power at the expense of some batting average.

With Mike Cameron in center, the Mariners will play Ichiro in right field. He should provide a spark from the leadoff spot that the team has lacked for years.

— **James Bailey**

MINOR LEAGUE MENTIONS BY BA

YEAR	TOP 100	ORG RANKING	LEAGUE RANKING	BEST TOOLS
2001	No. 9	**No. 2:** Mariners		

Complete Minor League Statistics, Including Short-Season Leagues

BaseBall america

AS IN
HERO

Ichiro and the Mariners are the
story of the season as
baseball heads to Seattle

MAJOR LEAGUE MIDSEASON UPDATE
Bold Predictions For The Second Half
Midseason Award Winners & All-Stars
Highs & Lows For Every Organization

MARK TEIXEIRA, 1B

BIOGRAPHY

PROPER NAME: Mark Charles Teixeira. **BORN:** April 11, 1980 in Annapolis, Md.
HT: 6-3. **WT:** 225. **BATS:** B. **THROWS:** R. **SCHOOL:** Georgia Tech.
FIRST PRO CONTRACT: Selected by Rangers in first round (fifth overall) of 2001 draft;
signed Aug. 24, 2001.

TEXAS RANGERS TOP 10 PROSPECTS FOR 2002

Teixeira turned down the Red Sox's seven-figure bonus offer out of high school as a ninth-rounder in 1998. He was the top prospect in the Cape Cod League in 1999 and Baseball America's College Player of the Year in 2000.

Despite missing most of his junior season at Georgia Tech with a fractured right ankle, he went fifth overall in the 2001 draft and signed for a major league contract worth $9.5 million.

Teixeira was both the best pure hitter and the best power hitter available in the 2001 draft, and he was the most advanced college bat since Pat Burrell went No. 1 overall in the 1998 draft. A switch-hitter, he is proficient from both sides of the plate.

Before he got hurt, he had made strides with his running and defense. He didn't play the field after returning from the injury, so there will be questions about his defense until he does. He still has to show he can play third base in the majors, though Hank Blalock's presence and Carlos Pena's trade will make it easier to move Teixeira to first base.

The injury and protracted contract negotiations left Teixeira rusty in instructional league, where he hit .246 with one homer in 57 at-bats. He'll stay at the hot corner for now and could debut as high as Double-A Tulsa.

— **Gerry Fraley**

MINOR LEAGUE MENTIONS BY BA

YEAR	TOP 100	ORG RANKING	LEAGUE RANKING	BEST TOOLS
2002	No. 10	**No. 2:** Rangers	**No. 1:** Florida State **No. 1:** Texas	**FSL:** Best Hitter
2003	No. 1	**No. 1:** Rangers		

MIGUEL TEJADA, SS

BIOGRAPHY

PROPER NAME: Miguel Odalis Tejada. **BORN:** May 25, 1974 in Bani, Dominican Republic. **HT:** 5-9. **WT:** 220. **BATS:** R. **THROWS:** R. **SCHOOL:** Bani, Dominican Republic. **FIRST PRO CONTRACT:** Signed as international free agent by Athletics, July 17, 1993.

NORTHWEST LEAGUE TOP 10 PROSPECTS FOR 1995

Not every manager tabbed the Dominican as his No. 1 prospect, but those who did weren't at all hesitant about it. His astonishing range at short had his own teammates shaking their heads, even late in the season.

Tejada's range and his ability to produce runs tagged him as the NWL player most likely to go the farthest in the shortest time.

"Good bat speed, good pitch selection, all the tools to be a good offensive player, and he can run," Portland manager P.J. Carey said. "He's a five-tool player, and you don't see those that often at this level."

— **Shannon Fears**

OAKLAND ATHLETICS TOP 10 PROSPECTS FOR 1996

BACKGROUND: Tejada was signed by Hall of Famer Juan Marichal, Oakland's director of Latin American scouting. Tejada led the DSL with 18 homers in 1994, gaining him distinction of becoming the first player from the Athletics' Dominican program to bypass the Rookie-level Arizona League. He responded by earning top prospect honors in the Northwest League last year.

STRENGTHS: Tejada is a legitimate shortstop with great range, fine hands and an above-average arm. Offensively, he has speed and power potential. The A's expect higher batting average as he matures.

WEAKNESSES: Tejada still makes his share of teenage mistakes. He swings and throws too hard. His 26 errors in 74 games were mostly on wild throws.

FUTURE: Tejada is heading for high Class A ball in Modesto.

— **Casey Tefertiller**

MINOR LEAGUE MENTIONS BY BA

YEAR	TOP 100	ORG RANKING	LEAGUE RANKING	BEST TOOLS
1995			**No. 1:** Northwest	
1996	No. 88	**No. 6:** Athletics	**No. 1:** California	**CAL:** Most Exciting Player
1997	No. 6	**No. 1:** Athletics	**No. 1:** Southern	**SL:** Best Defensive SS
1998	No. 10	**No. 2:** Athletics		

FRANK THOMAS, 1B

BIOGRAPHY

PROPER NAME: Frank Edward Thomas. **BORN:** May 27, 1968 in Columbus, Ga.
HT: 6-5. **WT:** 240. **BATS:** R. **THROWS:** R. **SCHOOL:** Auburn.
FIRST PRO CONTRACT: Selected by White Sox in first round (seventh overall)
of 1989 draft; signed June 11, 1989.

CHICAGO WHITE SOX TOP 10 PROSPECTS FOR 1990

Thomas was not the best talent available when the White Sox spent the seventh pick of June's draft. They took him because there was not a legitimate power prospect in the system, and he could be a 30-homer man someday. His swing might need to be tightened, but he had little trouble with Class A breaking balls. He is an ox at first base and likely will wind up a designated hitter.

— **Ken Leiker**

SOUTHERN LEAGUE TOP 10 PROSPECTS FOR 1990

Thomas, 22, almost bypassed the league this season. He had a sensational spring and was one of the White Sox's last cuts when they broke camp.

Instead of sulking about being sent down, Thomas went to Birmingham and went to work on league pitchers. His .545 slugging percentage and .476 on-base percentage (on the strength of 112 walks in 109 games) made it easy for the White Sox to bring him up in early August.

"He can hit for average, power and is good at getting on base," Birmingham manager Ken Berry said. "He still needs to work hard on his defense, baserunning and situational play, but those are things that come with experience."

— **Rubin Grant**

MINOR LEAGUE MENTIONS BY BA				
YEAR	**TOP 100**	**ORG RANKING**	**LEAGUE RANKING**	**BEST TOOLS**
1989			**No. 3:** Florida State	
1990	No. 29	**No. 7:** White Sox	**No. 1:** Southern	**SL:** Best Hitter, Best Power, Most Exciting Player

JIM THOME, 1B

BIOGRAPHY

PROPER NAME: James Howard Thome. **BORN:** August 27, 1970 in Peoria, Ill.
HT: 6-4. **WT:** 250. **BATS:** L. **THROWS:** R. **SCHOOL:** Illinois Central JC.
FIRST PRO CONTRACT: Selected by Indians in 13th round (333rd overall) of 1989 draft;
signed June 18, 1989.

APPALACHIAN LEAGUE TOP 10 PROSPECTS FOR 1990

In Thome's 34 games in the league, he put numbers on the board and fear in the hearts of opposing pitchers. He was on pace to contend for a triple crown before getting called to Kinston, where he hit .308 in 33 games.

"I saw him in instructional league last year and it didn't look like the same kid," Kingsport manager Jim Thrift said. "He has the ability to stay back and use the whole field. I have to give him credit for improving his defense, too."

— **Dean Gyorgy**

EASTERN LEAGUE TOP 10 PROSPECTS FOR 1991

How does a 13th-round selection two seasons out of junior college emerge as the best prospect in a Double-A league? With hard work and a near-insatiable thirst for the game.

"Coaching third base, you get a chance to talk to him, get inside his head," Harrisburg manager Mike Quade said. "He's always talking about situations. He's fearless at the plate and has a good idea of what he wants to do up there."

"He hits well, and even though he doesn't run real well, he's got a quick first step at third base," New Britain manager Gary Allenson said. "He's a line-drive hitter who has power potential, and he has a great mental outlook."

"He's turned into a plus defensive player," said Thome's own manager, Ken Bolek of Canton-Akron. "Offensively he's capable of hitting for a high average with power. He's going to improve his home run totals, and he has outstanding makeup. He's a gamer."

— **Bill Palmer**

MINOR LEAGUE MENTIONS BY BA

YEAR	TOP 100	ORG RANKING	LEAGUE RANKING	BEST TOOLS
1990			**No. 1:** Appalachian	
1991	No. 93	**No. 4:** Indians	**No. 1:** Eastern	**EL:** Best Hitter, Best Defensive 3B
1992	No. 51	**No. 4:** Indians		
1993			**No. 1:** International	**IL:** Best Hitter

MIKE TROUT, OF

2011 MiLB PLAYER OF THE YEAR

LOS ANGELES ANGELS TOP 10 PROSPECTS FOR 2010

A favorite of area scouts in the Northeast for his talent and makeup, Trout was the only player to appear at MLB Network's studios for the television broadcast of the draft last June. It wasn't a wasted trip. The Angels selected him 26th overall and signed him for $1.215 million. He rated as the Rookie-level Arizona League's No. 1 prospect and finished second in the batting race at .360.

Trout has a line-drive stroke, the ability to make adjustments and a refined batting eye. His strength and bat speed give him the potential for average power. As good as his feel for hitting is, his plus-plus speed stands out even more. He gets from home to first in 3.9 seconds from the right side, enabling him to leg out infield hits.

Built like a football defensive back, he has above-average range and instincts in center field. His arm is average. Trout hit only one home run in his pro debut and has yet to learn to pull the ball consistently. When using the opposite field, he tends to push the ball rather than drive through it.

Already listed at 200 pounds, he might fill out, slow down and move to an outfield corner. The Angels haven't developed a starting outfielder since Darin Erstad, so they were thrilled to grab Trout, believing he was overlooked as a high schooler from the Northeast. He'll take his well-rounded game and five-tool potential to low Class A Cedar Rapids in 2010.

— **Matt Eddy**

MINOR LEAGUE MENTIONS BY BA

YEAR	TOP 100	ORG RANKING	LEAGUE RANKING	BEST TOOLS
2009			**No. 1:** Arizona	
2010	No. 85	**No. 3:** Angels	**No. 1:** Midwest **No. 1:** California	**MWL:** Best Hitter, Best Baserunner, Fastest Baserunner, Best Defensive OF, Most Exciting Player
2011	No. 2	**No. 1:** Angels	**No. 1:** Texas	**TL:** Best Hitter, Best Baserunner, Best Defensive OF, Most Exciting Player
2012	No. 3	**No. 1:** Angels		

TROY TULOWITZKI, SS

BIOGRAPHY

PROPER NAME: Troy Trevor Tulowitzki. **BORN:** October 10, 1984 in Santa Clara, Calif.
HT: 6-3. **WT:** 205. **BATS:** R. **THROWS:** R. **SCHOOL:** Long Beach State.
FIRST PRO CONTRACT: Selected by Rockies in first round (seventh overall) of 2005 draft;
signed June 10, 2005.

COLORADO ROCKIES TOP 10 PROSPECTS FOR 2006

Tulowitzki has been compared to Bobby Crosby since succeeding him at shortstop for Long Beach State. The seventh overall pick in the 2005 draft, he signed for $2.3 million. He went straight to high Class A, and the only negative in his pro debut was a torn quadriceps that limited him to 22 games.

Most scouts think Tulowitzki is slightly ahead of Crosby, the 2004 American League Rookie of the Year, at the same stage of their careers and a better fit at shortstop. Tulowitzki has the stroke, strength and bat speed to hit 25-30 homers annually. Though he's big, he doesn't sacrifice any athleticism. He has above-average range and arm strength, and his exceptional instincts allow him to extend his range.

Tulowitzki sometimes can get out of control and too aggressive at the plate. He could control the strike zone a little better. A broken hamate bone in the spring and the torn quad restricted his development in 2005.

Despite the injury, Tulowitzki should be able to handle the jump to Double-A for his first full season. He could be Colorado's starter by 2007.

— **Tracy Ringolsby**

MINOR LEAGUE MENTIONS BY BA

YEAR	TOP 100	ORG RANKING	LEAGUE RANKING	BEST TOOLS
2006	No. 25	**No. 2:** Rockies	**No. 3:** Texas	**TL:** Best INF Arm
2007	No. 15	**No. 1:** Rockies		

CHASE UTLEY, 2B

BIOGRAPHY

PROPER NAME: Chase Cameron Utley. **BORN:** December 17, 1978 in Pasadena, Calif.
HT: 6-1. **WT:** 195. **BATS:** L. **THROWS:** R. **SCHOOL:** UCLA.
FIRST PRO CONTRACT: Selected by Phillies in first round (15th overall) of 2000 draft;
signed July 29, 2000.

PHILADELPHIA PHILLIES TOP 10 PROSPECTS FOR 2001

Drafted as a shortstop in the second round out of high school by the Dodgers, Utley spurned their offer to attend UCLA. He achieved All-America honors as a junior, batting .382 and leading the Pacific-10 Conference with 82 runs scored before the Phillies used the 15th overall pick and $1.7 million to sign him.

Utley was considered the best pure hitter available among college draft prospects, and he has plenty of sock for a middle infielder. He lived up to his reputation in his pro debut. He always has demonstrated a good idea of the strike zone and handles the bat well. Utley has drawn comparisons to Todd Walker (Rockies) and Adam Kennedy (Angels), two former first-round picks, based on both his offensive prowess and defensive shortcomings.

At the plate, Utley needs to use the whole field more effectively. He's improving in that regard by staying inside pitches better and driving them to left-center. He's adjusting to the finer points of playing second base and will have to prove he can stick there.

The Phillies envision Utley's bat fitting in nicely with their young nucleus in the near future. He's expected to begin a rapid ascent through the system by beginning 2001 in Clearwater

— **Josh Boyd**

MINOR LEAGUE MENTIONS BY BA

YEAR	TOP 100	ORG RANKING	LEAGUE RANKING	BEST TOOLS
2001		**No. 5:** Phillies	**No. 15:** Florida State	
2002		**No. 7:** Phillies	**No. 14:** International	
2003	No. 81	**No. 2:** Phillies	**No. 4:** International	**IL:** Best Hitter

ROBIN VENTURA, 3B

BIOGRAPHY

PROPER NAME: Robin Mark Ventura. **BORN:** July 14, 1967 in Santa Maria, Calif.
HT: 6-1. **WT:** 198. **BATS:** L. **THROWS:** R. **SCHOOL:** Oklahoma State.
FIRST PRO CONTRACT: Selected by White Sox in first round (10th overall) of 1988 draft;
signed Oct. 21, 1988.

CHICAGO WHITE SOX TOP 10 PROSPECTS FOR 1989

He was a lefthanded-hitting machine at Oklahoma State and the RBI leader on the U.S. Olympic team. Ventura should have no trouble adjusting to a wood bat, because he has a quick hands and a short swing. He is not a power hitter, but produces runs with a line-drive swing to all fields, and he has not shown susceptibility to any style of pitcher.

Ventura's only below-average grade is for running speed, but he upgrades that by rarely making a mistake on the bases.

Bat potential aside, the White Sox have an immediate opening for Ventura because their third baseman made 46 errors last season. He is not Brooks Robinson, but he is competent enough in all areas to make the plays that are supposed to be outs.

— **Ken Leiker**

CHICAGO WHITE SOX TOP 10 PROSPECTS FOR 1990

The hitting machine from Oklahoma State handled Double-A pitching in his first pro season and, despite 27 errors, convinced the White Sox he will be an adequate third baseman.

Some scouts say the Sox will have to be satisfied with a line-drive producer because Ventura doesn't have the swing to reach double figures in home runs. The Sox say it's too early to make that judgement.

— **Ken Leiker**

MINOR LEAGUE MENTIONS BY BA

YEAR	TOP 100	ORG RANKING	LEAGUE RANKING	BEST TOOLS
1989		**No. 1:** White Sox		**SL:** Best Defensive 3B
1990	No. 15	**No. 3:** White Sox		

FOCUS ON SPORT/GETTY IMAGES | ISSUE DATE: AUGUST, 1987

246

JUSTIN VERLANDER, RHP

BIOGRAPHY

PROPER NAME: Justin Brooks Verlander. **BORN:** February 20, 1983 in Manakin-Sabot, Va.
HT: 6-5. **WT:** 225. **BATS:** R. **THROWS:** R. **SCHOOL:** Old Dominion.
FIRST PRO CONTRACT: Selected by Tigers in first round (second overall) of 2004 draft;
signed Oct. 25, 2004.

DETROIT TIGERS TOP 10 PROSPECTS FOR 2005

Verlander had as electric an arm as anyone in the 2004 draft, though he went just 21-18 in three college seasons. The Tigers drafted him second overall, then broke off negotiations with him and his agent in October. Verlander's father jumpstarted the talks the following week, and Verlander signed a five-year big league contract with a $3.12 million bonus and $4.5 million guaranteed.

Equipped with a lightning-quick arm, Verlander regularly pitches in the mid-90s and touched 99 mph several times during the spring of his junior year. His curveball is a knee-buckling hammer with vicious downward bite, and his changeup could give him a third plus pitch.

The Tigers will have to make up for lost time and start reshaping Verlander's delivery when he reports to spring training. His command is affected by his upright finish and short stride, which causes him to leave too many pitches up in the zone. He doesn't use his changeup as much as he should.

Verlander has the stuff to front a rotation, but scouts are divided on whether he profiles better as a closer. Detroit hopes he'll remain a starter and will begin his career in high Class A.

— **Pat Caputo**

MINOR LEAGUE MENTIONS BY BA

YEAR	TOP 100	ORG RANKING	LEAGUE RANKING	BEST TOOLS
2005		**No. 3:** Tigers	**No. 2:** Florida State	**FSL:** Best Pitching Prospect, Best Fastball, Best Breaking Pitch, Best Control
2006	No. 8	**No. 1:** Tigers		

Baseball America

MAJORS • MINORS • PROSPECTS • DRAFT • COLLEGE • HIGH SCHOOL

Take An Inside Look At Major League Baseball's Scout School

Part One Of Our Review Of The 2005 Draft: Who Signed And Who Didn't

Baylor Tops Our Annual Rankings Of College Recruiting Classes

We thought last season's collection was strong, but this year's group of rookies—led by Rookie of the Year Justin Verlander—might be the best ever.

BUMPER
CROP 2
THE SEQUEL

OMAR VIZQUEL, SS

BIOGRAPHY

PROPER NAME: Omar Enrique Vizquel. **BORN:** April 24, 1967 in Caracas, Venezuela.
HT: 5-9. **WT:** 180. **BATS:** B. **THROWS:** R. **SCHOOL:** Francisco Espejo, Venezuela.
FIRST PRO CONTRACT: Signed as international free agent by Mariners, April 1, 1984.

SEATTLE MARINERS TOP 10 PROSPECTS FOR 1988

Signed as a 16-year-old out of Venezuela in 1984, Vizquel was used sparingly in his first two pro seasons (232 at-bats in 1984 and 1985), but he has picked up the pace the last two years and made dramatic improvement in 1987.

He is still physically maturing and will get stronger with the bat—although his power will be measured in doubles, not home runs. He still has to learn when to run, but the basestealing potential is there.

— Tracy Ringolsby

EASTERN LEAGUE TOP 10 PROSPECTS FOR 1988

Vizquel made the list for his proficiency with the glove, though he showed signs of coming of age with the bat and on the bases. His knowledge of the game belies his age (21). Not only does he have great range and a strong throwing arm, but he played the hitters better than anyone in the league.

"After everyone else has gone in the clubhouse, Omar's out here watching [the opponents] hit," said Vermont manager Rich Morales. "He just sits there and watches and picks up a lot of things that way."

— Kevin Iole

MINOR LEAGUE MENTIONS BY BA

YEAR	TOP 100	ORG RANKING	LEAGUE RANKING	BEST TOOLS
1987				**CAR:** Best Defensive SS
1988		**No. 8:** Mariners	**No. 4:** Eastern	**EL:** Best Defensive SS
1989		**No. 5:** Mariners		

JOEY VOTTO, 1B

BIOGRAPHY

PROPER NAME: Joseph Daniel Votto. **BORN:** September 10, 1983 in Toronto.
HT: 6-2. **WT:** 220. **BATS:** L. **THROWS:** R. **SCHOOL:** Richview Collegiate Institute, Toronto.
FIRST PRO CONTRACT: Selected by Reds in second round (44th overall) of 2002 draft;
signed Oct. 25, 2004.

CINCINNATI REDS TOP 10 PROSPECTS FOR 2007

Votto bounced back from a difficult 2005 season to emerge as the Double-A Southern League's MVP last year. He led the SL in batting (.319), on-base percentage (.408) and slugging (.547), as well as runs (85), hits (162), total bases (278), extra-base hits (70), doubles (46) and walks (78).

Votto has the ability to drive the ball to all fields, especially to left-center when he's locked in. His hands are quick enough that he can punish pitchers if they try to bust him inside. A hard worker, Votto devoted time to his baserunning and stole 24 bases in 31 tries last year despite average speed.

A catcher when he signed, Votto is still a little raw at first base. He sometimes goes too far into the hole on balls, leaving him out of position. He also can improve his footwork and throwing accuracy. Like many young lefthanded hitters, he struggles against southpaws.

Votto is the Reds' first baseman of the future—and that future could begin as soon as this year. He'll head to Triple-A and be in line for a September call-up, though he could accelerate that timetable with a strong start.

— J.J. Cooper

MINOR LEAGUE MENTIONS BY BA

YEAR	TOP 100	ORG RANKING	LEAGUE RANKING	BEST TOOLS
2003		**No. 14:** Reds	**No. 10:** Pioneer	
2004		**No. 5:** Reds	**No. 7:** Midwest	
2005		**No. 4:** Reds		
2006		**No. 9:** Reds	**No. 7:** Southern	**SL:** Best Hitter, Best Defensive 1B
2007	No. 43	**No. 3:** Reds	**No. 10:** International	**IL:** Best Hitter, Best Strike-Zone Judgment
2008	No. 44	**No. 3:** Reds		

BILLY WAGNER, LHP

BIOGRAPHY

PROPER NAME: William Edward Wagner. **BORN:** July 25, 1971 in Tannersville, Va.
HT: 5-10. **WT:** 180. **BATS:** L. **THROWS:** L. **SCHOOL:** Ferrum (Va.) College.
FIRST PRO CONTRACT: Selected by the Astros in first round (12th overall) of 1993 draft;
signed June 22, 1993.

TEXAS LEAGUE TOP 10 PROSPECTS FOR 1995

During a short stay, Wagner dominated the league. The power pitcher left for Triple-A Tucson shortly before midseason, leaving an impression on Texas League managers and hitters before he left.

Wagner's fastball is his best weapon. He needs work on his curveball and changeup. With command of those pitches, he could be an All-Star.

"He just has an overpowering fastball," Jackson manager Tim Tolman said. "His command and his ability to throw the fastball to spots when he needed it was why he dominated. He's a consistent curveball away from the majors."

— George Schroeder

PACIFIC COAST LEAGUE TOP 10 PROSPECTS FOR 1996

Though Wagner was in Houston by June, he had already left his mark as one of the PCL's top lefthanders. The reputation of his fastball is well-known. His composure and maturity also impressed managers.

"He's one of the best power pitchers I've seen," Phoenix manager Ron Wotus said. "His fastball is impressive, and he combines that with an effective changeup. I think in the years to come we'll be hearing a lot about this guy. He conducts himself as a professional."

Wagner was a starter for Tucson, but became an effective closer for Houston. One of his highlights was striking out Barry Bonds and Matt Williams with the bases loaded in the ninth inning to save a win over San Francisco.

— Javier Morales

MINOR LEAGUE MENTIONS BY BA				
YEAR	**TOP 100**	**ORG RANKING**	**LEAGUE RANKING**	**BEST TOOLS**
1994	No. 78	**No. 3:** Astros	**No. 2:** Midwest	**MWL:** Best Pitching Prospect, Best Fastball
1995	No. 17	**No. 2:** Astros	**No. 2:** Texas	**TL:** Best Pitching Prospect, Best Fastball
1996	No. 14	**No. 1:** Astros	**No. 3:** Pacific Coast	**PCL:** Best Pitching Prospect

SPORTING NEWS VIA GETTY IMAGES VIA GETTY IMAGES | ISSUE DATE: JANUARY, 1996

ADAM WAINWRIGHT, RHP

BIOGRAPHY

PROPER NAME: Adam Parrish Wainwright. **BORN:** August 30, 1981 in Brunswick, Ga.
HT: 6-7. **WT:** 235. **BATS:** R. **THROWS:** R. **SCHOOL:** Glynn Academy, Brunswick, Ga.
FIRST PRO CONTRACT: Selected by Braves in first round (29th overall) of 2000 draft;
signed June 12, 2000.

ATLANTA BRAVES TOP 10 PROSPECTS FOR 2001

The Braves targeted Wainwright throughout the spring as the 29th overall pick in the 2000 draft. He breezed through the Rookie-level Gulf Coast League before receiving a promotion to the Appalachian League after seven starts. He left no doubt why he was a first-rounder, ranking as the Appy League's top prospect and second-best in the GCL.

For a teenager, Wainwright's overall command and ability to throw strikes with his changeup is uncanny. He's mature and competitive. In addition to a plus changeup, Wainwright features a low-90s fastball and an average curveball. His maturity can overshadow his inexperience against professional hitters.

He wore down in late August and must improve his strength in order to pitch at a high level for a full season. Added strength should add velocity to his four-seam fastball.

The progress Wainwright made last season will enable him to open 2001 at Macon. The Braves say that finding the right place to challenge Wainwright at this point in his career could be the most difficult decision.

— **Javier Morales**

MINOR LEAGUE MENTIONS BY BA

YEAR	TOP 100	ORG RANKING	LEAGUE RANKING	BEST TOOLS
2000			**No. 2:** Gulf Coast **No. 1:** Appalachian	
2001	No. 97	**No. 7:** Braves	**No. 3:** South Atlantic	**SAL:** Best Pitching Prospect
2002	No. 42	**No. 2:** Braves	**No. 3:** Carolina	**CAR:** Best Fastball
2003	No. 18	**No. 1:** Braves	**No. 13:** Southern	
2004	No. 49	**No. 2:** Cardinals		
2005		**No. 2:** Cardinals		
2006		**No. 6:** Cardinals		

LARRY WALKER, OF

BIOGRAPHY

PROPER NAME: Larry Kenneth Robert Walker.
BORN: December 1, 1966 in Maple Ridge, Canada.
HT: 6-3. **WT:** 215. **BATS:** L. **THROWS:** R. **SCHOOL:** Maple Ridge (Canada) HS.
FIRST PRO CONTRACT: Signed as international free agent by Montreal Expos, Nov. 14, 1984.

MIDWEST LEAGUE TOP 10 PROSPECTS FOR 1986

The Expos are drooling over this Canadian-born power hitter. Signed as a raw talent out of Maple Ridge, B.C., last summer, Walker hit just .223 with two homers at Utica (New York-Penn) in his pro debut.

Somehow, over the winter, Walker became a monster. The 19-year-old batted .290 in 95 games at Burlington, mashing 29 homers and driving in 74 runs. That forced the Expos to move Walker to West Palm Beach (Florida State), where he hit .283 with four more homers in 38 games.

Although some say he needs to make more contact—112 strikeouts in 331 at-bats—the biggest knock against Walker is that he lacks a position. He was tried at third base, then shifted to left field. That should become his home.

"He has major league power," Springfield manager Gaylen Pitts said. "Anyone who can hit like that, you find him a place to play."

One manager predicted Walker would hit 30 homers a year in the big leagues.

— Jon Scher

MINOR LEAGUE MENTIONS BY BA

YEAR	TOP 100	ORG RANKING	LEAGUE RANKING	BEST TOOLS
1986			**No. 2:** Midwest	**MWL:** Best Hitter, Best Power
1987		**No. 9:** Expos	**No. 3:** Southern	
1988		**No. 5:** Expos		
1989		**No. 3:** Expos	**No. 3:** American Association	**AA:** Best OF Arm

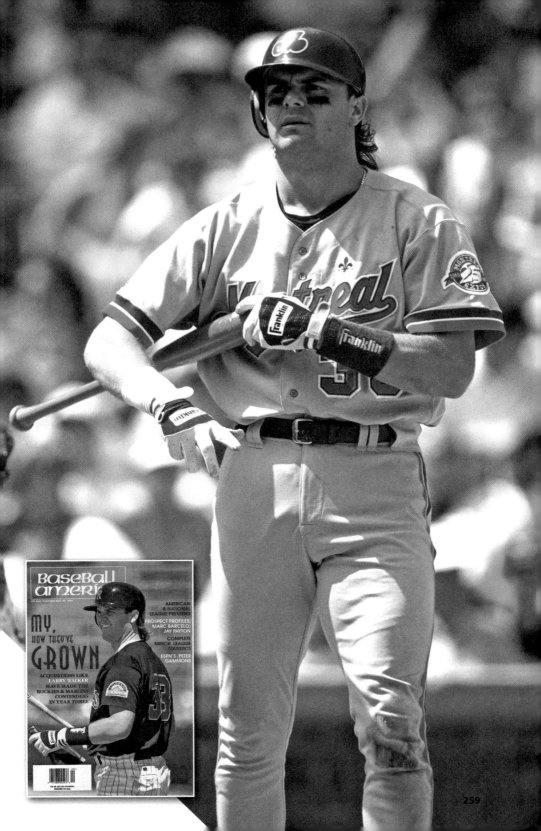

JERED WEAVER, RHP

BIOGRAPHY

PROPER NAME: Jered David Weaver. **BORN:** October 4, 1982 in Northridge, Calif.
HT: 6-7. **WT:** 210. **BATS:** R. **THROWS:** R. **SCHOOL:** Long Beach State.
FIRST PRO CONTRACT: Selected by Angels in first round (12th overall) of 2004 draft; signed May 31, 2005.

LOS ANGELES ANGELS TOP 10 PROSPECTS FOR 2006

BACKGROUND: Weaver had one of the most dominant college seasons ever in 2004, going 15-1, 1.63 with 213 strikeouts in 144 innings to win Baseball America's College Player of the Year award. The top-rated prospect for the 2004 draft, he dropped to the Angels at No. 12 because of concerns about his price tag. Weaver held out until a week before the 2005 draft before agreeing to a $4 million bonus. He reached Double-A in his pro debut and later pitched in the Arizona Fall League and the Olympic regional qualifier. His brother Jeff has won 78 big league games in the last seven seasons.

STRENGTHS: Weaver owns the system's best combination of present stuff and command. His arm is loose and fast, and he works from a three-quarter arm slot slightly higher than that of his brother. He relies on a nasty, 86-90 mph two-seam fastball, a 91-93 mph four-seamer, a slider and a changeup. He pitches with tenacity and passion. Weaver's command is more notable than his stuff, and some scouts think he's more of a No. 3 starter than a headliner.

WEAKNESSES: He's an extreme flyball pitcher and is vulnerable to homers. His slider grades as an above-average pitch at times but lack consistency. A free spirit, he loses his cool at times.

FUTURE: Some hyperbolic scouting reports declared Weaver as big league-ready when he entered pro ball, but he is at least another half-season away from joining the Angels. He'll open 2006 in Triple-A.

— **Alan Matthews**

MINOR LEAGUE MENTIONS BY BA

YEAR	TOP 100	ORG RANKING	LEAGUE RANKING	BEST TOOLS
2006	No. 57	**No. 5:** Angels	**No. 2:** Pacific Coast	**PCL:** Best Pitching Prospect

BRANDON WEBB, RHP

BIOGRAPHY

PROPER NAME: Brandon Tyler Webb. **BORN:** May 9, 1979 in Ashland, Ky.
HT: 6-3. **WT:** 230. **BATS:** R. **THROWS:** R. **SCHOOL:** Kentucky.
FIRST PRO CONTRACT: Selected by D-backs in eighth round (249th overall) of 2000 draft;
signed June 6, 2000.

ARIZONA DIAMONDBACKS TOP 10 PROSPECTS FOR 2003

Webb set the Kentucky single-season strikeout record (since broken by Athletics first-rounder Joe Blanton) in 2000, the year Arizona drafted him in the eighth round. After being shut down with a tired arm in his first pro summer, he has been solid ever since. He ranked fourth in the Texas League in both ERA and strikeouts last year.

Webb's fastball tops out at 94-95 mph but is best at 92 mph, where it really sinks. He also has a heavy slider, and his stuff reminds scouts of Bob Wickman's. His two-seam fastball can be so dominant that he could rely on it almost exclusively.

With 40 hit batters and 23 wild pitches over the last two seasons, it's obvious Webb still has work to do to master his command. His pitches have such live, late movement that he can be difficult to catch. He just began to incorporate a changeup into his repertoire last year.

Like his former El Paso teammate Mike Gosling, Webb has an outside chance to make the D-backs roster in 2003. He could be used as either a starter or a long reliever. Whatever the case, he should be a major league mainstay in the near future.

— **Jack Magruder**

MINOR LEAGUE MENTIONS BY BA

YEAR	TOP 100	ORG RANKING	LEAGUE RANKING	BEST TOOLS
2001		**No. 27:** D-backs		
2002		**No. 26:** D-backs		
2003		**No. 5:** D-backs		

Baseball For The Ages: Our Annual Look At The Best Players From 12 To 25

BaseBallamerica

Arizona's Brandon Webb
emerges from obscurity
to become our
Rookie of the Year

WEBB
GEM

Top 20 Rookies

Updated Draft List, Including Every Signing

First Reports From Arizona Fall League

DAVID WRIGHT, 3B

BIOGRAPHY

PROPER NAME: David Allen Wright. **BORN:** December 20, 1982 in Norfolk, Va.
HT: 6-0. **WT:** 205. **BATS:** R. **THROWS:** R. **SCHOOL:** Hickory HS, Chesapeake, Va.
FIRST PRO CONTRACT: Selected by Mets in first round (38th overall) of 2001 draft; signed July 12, 2001.

NEW YORK METS TOP 10 PROSPECTS FOR 2002

Wright was considered one of the best high school hitters available in the 2001 draft. He adjusted to wood bats easily, with consistent line drives to the gaps. Wright has a strong body, quick wrists and improving swing extension that should allow him to hit for both power and average as his body matures.

Many scouts say he has the ability and approach to hit .300 with 30 home runs in the major leagues. He's aggressive and has good mobility at third base. He also runs well for a player his size, and Appalachian League observers raved about his work ethic. Wright simply needs to face better pitching to continue his maturation as a hitter.

While some wonder if he can stay at third base, he has the instincts and athleticism to move to a corner outfield position if necessary.

Few teams are more conservative with young players than the Mets. With a solid debut under his belt, Wright is expected to move to Capital City in 2002 and should move up this list soon.

— **Bill Ballew**

MINOR LEAGUE MENTIONS BY BA

YEAR	TOP 100	ORG RANKING	LEAGUE RANKING	BEST TOOLS
2001			**No. 9:** Appalachian	
2002		**No. 5:** Mets	**No. 10:** South Atlantic	
2003	No. 75	**No. 4:** Mets	**No. 10:** Florida State	**FSL:** Best Defensive 3B
2004	No. 21	**No. 3:** Mets	**No. 1:** Eastern	**EL:** Best Hitter, Best Strike-Zone Judgment, Best Defensive 3B, Most Exciting Player

BaseBall america

MAJORS • MINORS • PROSPECTS • DRAFT • COLLEGE • HIGH SCHOOL

It wasn't long for Mets prospect David Wright to go from the Futures Game to New York

We Blanket Houston For Complete Futures Game Coverage

Visa Limit Creates Headaches For Foreign Players

Jason Kubel Highlights Another Raft Of Prospect Features

Triple-A All-Stars Light Up Pawtucket

THE FUTURE IS NOW

CHRISTIAN YELICH, OF

BIOGRAPHY

PROPER NAME: Christian Stephen Yelich. **BORN:** December 5, 1991 in Thousand Oaks, Calif.
HT: 6-3. **WT:** 195. **BATS:** L. **THROWS:** R. **SCHOOL:** Westlake HS, Westlake Village, Calif.
FIRST PRO CONTRACT: Selected by Marlins in first round (23rd overall) of 2010 draft;
signed Aug. 16, 2010.

FLORIDA MARLINS TOP 10 PROSPECTS FOR 2011

Yelich comes from the same Westlake High (Westlake Village, Calif.) program that produced big leaguers Matt Franco, Mike Lieberthal and John Snyder, as well as fellow Marlins farmhand Graham Johnson. Yelich produced against top competition in high school and on the showcase circuit, propelling him to the No. 23 overall pick in the 2010 draft. He signed an above-slot $1.7 million deal at the Aug. 16 signing deadline and reached low Class A in his brief pro debut.

Yelich has an advanced approach for a high school hitter, with smooth swing mechanics that have elicited comparisons to Will Clark's. He reads pitches well and projects as a high-average hitter with average power. Lefthanders don't bother him.

Though Yelich played first base at Westlake, he has slightly above-average speed and moved to left field in pro ball. The Marlins will try him in center field in 2011, though he'll likely settle on a corner. His arm was a question going into the draft, but Florida tweaked his mechanics and believes his throwing can become at least close to average.

Yelich will return to Greensboro to begin his first full season. After witnessing how seamlessly he transitioned to pro ball last year, the Marlins won't be afraid to move him should his bat warrant another jump. He should arrive in Florida by 2013.

— **James Bailey**

MINOR LEAGUE MENTIONS BY BA

YEAR	TOP 100	ORG RANKING	LEAGUE RANKING	BEST TOOLS
2011		**No. 3:** Marlins	**No. 5:** South Atlantic	
2012	No. 41	**No. 1:** Marlins	**No. 4:** Florida State	**FSL:** Most Exciting Player
2013	No. 15	**No. 2:** Marlins	**No. 5:** Southern	**SL:** Best Batting Prospect

BARRY ZITO, LHP

BIOGRAPHY

PROPER NAME: Barry William Zito. **BORN:** May 13, 1978 in Las Vegas.
HT: 6-2. **WT:** 205. **BATS:** L. **THROWS:** L. **SCHOOL:** Southern California.
FIRST PRO CONTRACT: Selected by Athletics in first round (ninth overall) of 1999 draft;
signed June 12, 1999.

CALIFORNIA LEAGUE TOP 10 PROSPECTS FOR 1999

Fresh from a dominant college season, Zito was one of the few phenoms quickly ushered in and out of the California League. Zito spent less than two months with the Oaks after signing with Oakland in June, and eventually helped Vancouver win the Triple-A World Series.

Zito continued his confident ways by piling up strikeouts and missing bats—opponents hit .156 against him—relying on his big-moving curveball and good command.

"Attitude and makeup, that's why he'll make it," Visalia manager Juan Navarette said. "He's a fierce competitor, loves to challenge hitters and is one of the smartest, most dedicated players I've ever come across. When I see that kind of desire with those kind of tools, all I can think is can't-miss."

— **Lance Pugmire**

PACIFIC COAST LEAGUE TOP 10 PROSPECTS FOR 2000

Zito went ninth overall in the 1999 draft in part because he was expected to reach the major leagues quickly. He exceeded even the most optimistic expectations, finishing his first pro season in the Triple-A World Series and making it to Oakland in July. After giving up a total of one run in his last five PCL starts, he was one of the American League's top pitchers down the stretch.

Zito, at 89 mph, doesn't have nearly the fastball that [Tacoma lefthander Ryan] Anderson has. But that's still good velocity for a lefthander, and Zito has everything else he needs to succeed. Though he has very good command of his pitches, he needs to cut down on his walks somewhat, but his refusal to give in makes him very difficult to hit.

— **Jim Callis**

MINOR LEAGUE MENTIONS BY BA

YEAR	TOP 100	ORG RANKING	LEAGUE RANKING	BEST TOOLS
1999			No. 4: California	
2000	No. 41	No. 2: Athletics	No. 2: Pacific Coast	PCL: Best Breaking Pitch

PHOTO CREDITS

Carl Kline. **PAGE 141:** Manny Machado by G Fiume/Getty Images. BA cover photo by Tom DiPace. **PAGE 143:** Greg Maddux by Focus on Sport/Getty Images. BA cover by Tom DiPace. **PAGE 145:** Russell Martin by Rob Tringali/Sportschrome/Getty Images. BA cover photo by Rick Battle. **PAGE 147:** Edgar Martinez by Ron Vesely/MLB Photos via Getty Images. **PAGE 149:** Pedro Martinez by Focus on Sport/Getty Images. BA cover photo by Steve Babineau/MLB photos. **PAGE 151:** Don Mattingly by Owen C. Shaw/Getty Images. BA cover photo by Tom DiPace (Mass) and Bruce Schwartzman (Mattingly.) **PAGE 153:** Joe Mauer by Larry Goren/Icon SMI/Icon Sport Media via Getty Images. BA cover photo by Linda Cullen. **PAGE 155:** Brian McCann by Brian Bahr/Getty Images. **PAGE 157:** Andrew McCutchen by Ronald C. Modra/Sports Imagery/Getty Images. BA cover photo by George Gojkovich. **PAGE 159:** Jack McDowell by Ron Vesely/MLB Photos via Getty Images. **PAGE 161:** Fred McGriff by Focus on Sport/Getty Images. **PAGE 163:** Mark McGwire by Focus on Sport/Getty Images. BA cover photo courtesy Oakland Athletics. **PAGE 165:** Yadier Molina by George Gojkovich/Getty Images. **PAGE 167:** Mike Mussina by Mitchell Layton/Getty Images. BA cover photo by Ron Vesely. **PAGE 169:** David Ortiz by Sporting News via Getty Images. **PAGE 171:** Roy Oswalt by Mitchell Layton/Getty Images. BA cover photo by Larry Goren. **PAGE 173:** Jake Peavy by Harry How/Getty Images. **PAGE 175:** Dustin Pedroia by Jim McIsaac/Getty Images. **PAGE 177:** Andy Pettitte by John G. Mabanglo/Afp/Getty Images **PAGE 179:** Mike Piazza by Ronald C. Modra/Sports Imagery/Getty Images. BA cover photo by Ron Vesely. **PAGE 181:** Jorge Posada by David Seelig/Allsport **PAGE 183:** Buster Posey by Brad Mangin/MLB Photos via Getty Images. BA cover photo by Larry Goren. **PAGE 185:** David Price by Jamie Squire/Getty Images. BA cover photo by Tom DiPace. **PAGE 187:** Kirby Puckett by Focus on Sport/Getty Images. BA cover photo courtesy Minnesota Twins. **PAGE 189:** Albert Pujols by Rich Pilling/MLB Photos via Getty Images. BA cover photo by John Williamson. **PAGE 191:** Manny Ramirez by Focus on Sport/Getty Images. BA cover photo by David L. Greene. **PAGE 193:** Mariano Rivera by Mitchell Layton/Getty Images. **PAGE 195:** Alex Rodriguez by Jonathan Daniel/Getty Images. BA cover photo by Tom DiPace. **PAGE 197:** Francisco Rodriguez by Brian Bahr/Getty Images. BA cover photo by Larry Goren. **PAGE 199:** Ivan Rodriguez by Focus on Sport/Getty Images. BA cover photo by Ron Vesely. **PAGE 201:** Scott Rolen by Mitchell Layton/Getty Images **PAGE 203:** Jimmy Rollins by Rick Stewart/Allsport. **PAGE 205:** C. C. Sabathia by David Maxwell/AFP/Getty Images. **PAGE 207:** Bret Saberhagen by Focus on Sport/Getty Images. **PAGE 209:** Chris Sale by Mark Cunningham/MLB Photos via Getty Images. BA cover photo by Ron Vesley. **PAGE 211:** Johan Santana by Tom Mihalek/AFP/Getty Images. **PAGE 213:** Max Scherzer by Jonathan Willey/Arizona Diamondbacks/MLB Photos via Getty Images. **PAGE 215:** Curt Schilling by Mitchell Layton/Getty Images. **PAGE 217:** Gary Sheffield by Focus on Sport/Getty Images. **PAGE 219:** John Smoltz by Focus on Sport/Getty Images. BA cover photo by Tom DiPace. **PAGE 221:** Blake Snell by Cliff Welch/Icon Sportswire via Getty Images. **PAGE 223:** Sammy Sosa by Focus on Sport/Getty Images. **PAGE 225:** Giancarlo Stanton by Mitchell Layton/Getty Images. BA cover photo by Jerry Hale. **PAGE 227:** Stephen Strasburg by Mark Goldman/Icon SMI/Corbis via Getty Images. BA cover photo by Jesse Soll. **PAGE 229:** Darryl Strawberry by Focus on Sport/Getty Images. **PAGE 231:** Ichiro Suzuki by John G. Mabanglo/AFP/Getty Images. BA cover photo by Larry Goren. **PAGE 233:** Mark Teixeira by John Williamson/MLB Photos via Getty Images. BA cover photo by Robert Gurganus. **PAGE 235:** Miguel Tejada by Jeff Carlick/Allsport. **PAGE 237:** Frank Thomas by Focus on Sport/Getty Images. BA cover photo by Bruce Schwartzman. **PAGE 239:** Jim Thome by Ron Vesely/MLB Photos via Getty Images. **PAGE 241:** Mike Trout by Jeff Gross/Getty Images. BA cover photo by David Stoner. **PAGE 243:** Troy Tulowitzki by Brad Mangin/MLB Photos via Getty Images. BA cover photo by David Stoner. **PAGE 245:** Chase Utley by Al Bello/Getty Images. **PAGE 247:** Robin Ventura by Focus on Sport/Getty Images. **PAGE 249:** Justin Verlander by Mark Cunningham/MLB Photos via Getty Images. BA cover photo by Tom DiPace. **PAGE 251:** Omar Vizquel by Focus on Sport/Getty Images. **PAGE 253:** Joey Votto by Brad Mangin/MLB Photos via Getty Images. **PAGE 255:** Billy Wagner by Sporting News via Getty Images. BA cover photo by Tom DiPace. **PAGE 257:** Adam Wainwright by Matthew Kutz/Sporting News via Getty Images. **PAGE 259:** Larry Walker by Focus on Sport/Getty Images. BA cover photo by Michael Ponzini. **PAGE 261:** Jered Weaver by Stephen Dunn/Getty Images. BA cover photo by Larry Goren. **PAGE 263:** Brandon Webb by Justin Sullivan/Getty Images. BA cover photo by Larry Goren. **PAGE 265:** David Wright by Brad Mangin/MLB Photos via Getty Images. BA cover photo by David Schofield. **PAGE 267:** Christian Yelich by Mitchell Layton/Getty Images. **PAGE 269:** Barry Zito by Jed Jacobsohn/Allsport.